A Childhood in Prison

PYOTR YAKIR

A CHILDHOOD IN PRISON

*Edited with
an Introduction by*
ROBERT CONQUEST

Coward, McCann & Geoghegan, Inc.
New York

First American Edition 1973

A Childhood in Prison Copyright © 1972 by Macmillan London Ltd.

Introduction, Notes and Appendix 1 Copyright © 1972 by Robert Conquest

All rights reserved. This book, or parts thereof, may not be reproduced in any form without permission in writing from the publisher.

SBN 698–10506–0
Library of Congress Catalog Card Number 72–86881

Printed in Great Britain by
RICHARD CLAY (THE CHAUCER PRESS), LTD., *Bungay, Suffolk*

Contents

Introduction by Robert Conquest   *page* 11

A CHILDHOOD IN PRISON by Pyotr Yakir

1. My Father's Arrest: Astrakhan   23
2. In Transit   63
3. The Verkhoturie Colony   89
4. Nizhnyaya Tura   105
5. Sevurallag   117

Appendix 1: The Execution of Pyotr Yakir's Father, by Robert Conquest   141

Appendix 2: Article 58 of the Criminal Code of the RSFR   145

Index   153

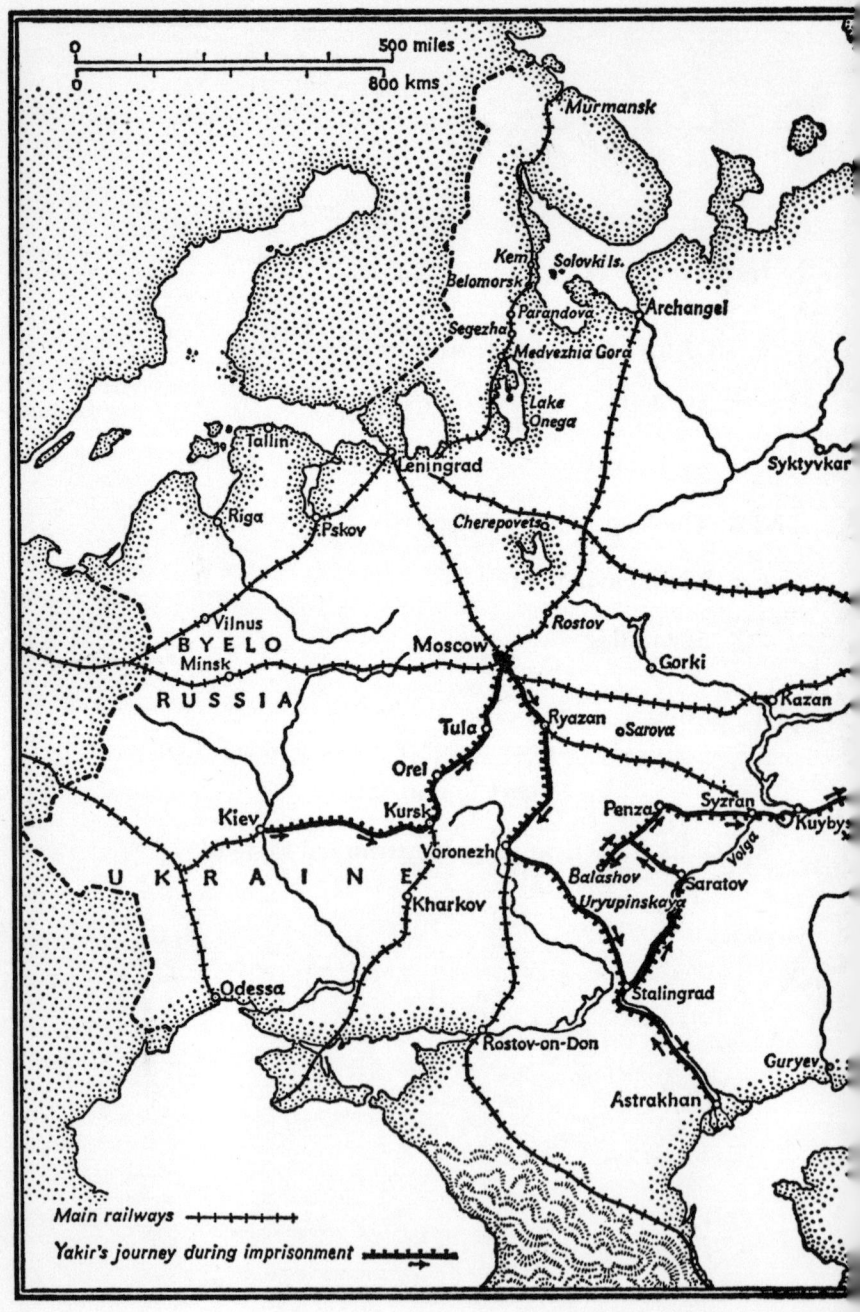

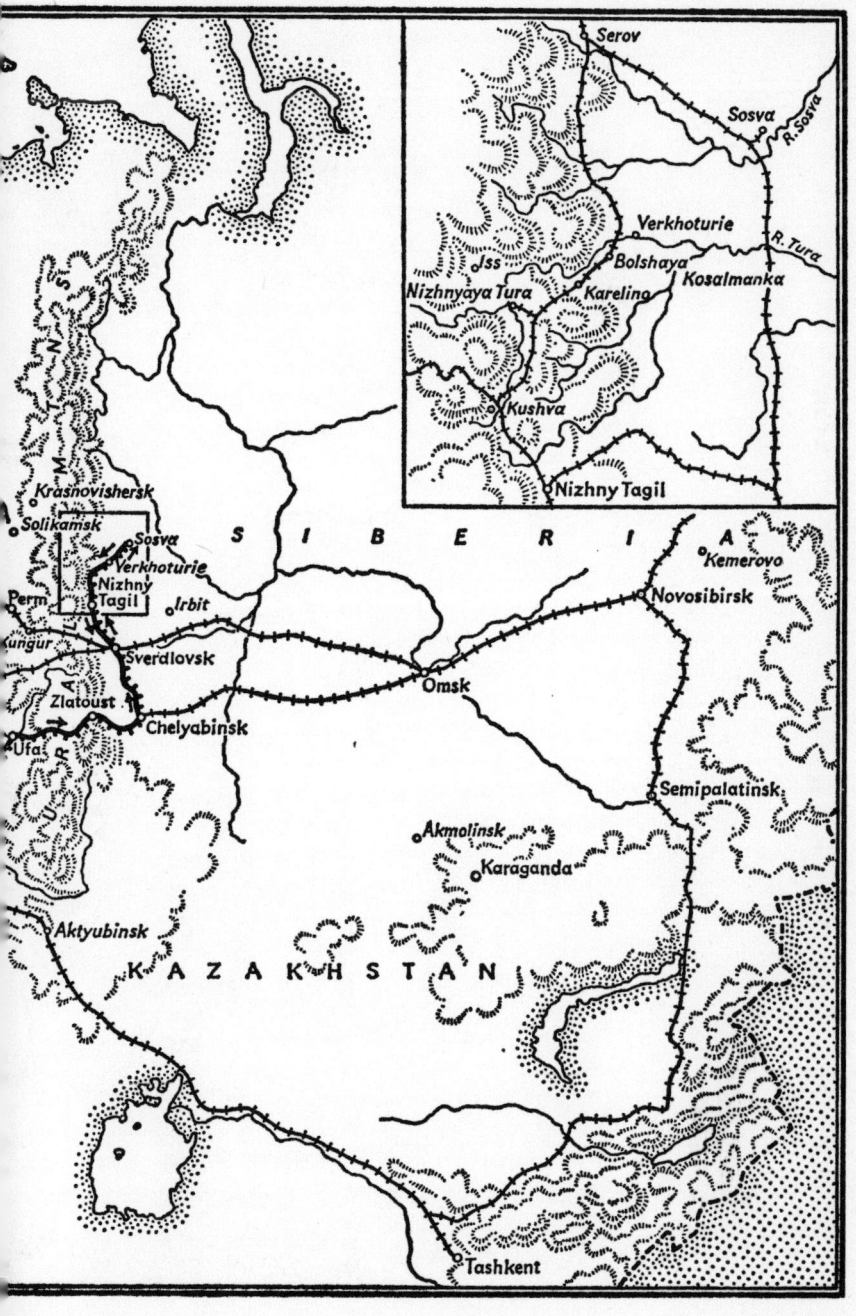

*Introduction
by
Robert Conquest*

Pyotr Yakir has written a very remarkable book, on more than one count. For the first time we are given a first-hand record of the experiences of a boy, orphaned by the firing squad, in Stalin's prisons and labour camps. The tone is almost always cool and objective, conveying without sentimentality the attitudes of a boy with sensible and healthy instincts but submitted to, and to some extent taking the colour of, a violent and vicious entourage. He recounts the squalor and the corruption, the tortures which he saw and to which he was himself submitted, without emotionalism. And he also tells us touchingly of the handful of good-hearted and intelligent men and women even there, who gave him a basis for the true elements of education, in their standards of decency and of thought.

In spite of the attempt to charge him with forming a band of Anarchist cavalry, in the event Pyotr Yakir was sentenced only as a 'Socially Dangerous Element'. That is to say, his only crime was being the son of his father, Army Commander Ion Yakir, shot on false charges on 12 June 1937.

He was, up to a point, lucky.

Under the decree of 7 April 1935, children over twelve could be shot: and in some cases they were. For example, the fourteen-year-old son of Nestor Lakoba, the Georgian Communist, was so executed. And when the last of the ex-Trotskyites and other genuine oppositionists were shot in the camps in 1938, the killing extended down to twelve-year-olds.

In general, the Secret Police had little mercy for the young. There was even one case (later disavowed), the celebrated Children's Plot in the town of Leninsk-Kuznetsk, in which

160 children down to ten years old, though mainly between twelve and fourteen, were arrested, were severely interrogated, and confessed to espionage, terror, treason and links with the Gestapo. (One ten-year-old broke down after a single night-long interrogation, admitting to membership of a Fascist organisation from the age of seven.)

If this book is unique in being the only account we have of a boy's experiences in the camps, it is unique too in being our only first-hand record by one who suffered directly through the liquidation of one of Stalin's major victims. That is to say, almost all the other first-hand accounts are like those of Evgenia Ginsburg or Alexander Weissberg, swept away by the almost accidental workings of the mass purge.

The event which destroyed Yakir's parents, wrecked his own young life, and in the long run transformed him into a powerful witness to truth and humanity in an oppressive system, was Stalin's great purge of the Red Army, which was launched at the 1937 trial and execution of Marshal Tukhachevsky, Army Commander Yakir and other senior Army officers. Pyotr Yakir provides in this book a number of hitherto unknown details about this massacre; I have given a more general account of the whole affair in an appendix. (On one other very important case of which the full story has never been told – the murder of Sergei Kirov on 1 December 1934 – Yakir also provides the historian with interesting new evidence, obtained from police officials and 'judges' involved.)

Mr Yakir's account of his teens spent in prison and camp speaks for itself. But the author's career after the expiration of his original sentence in the autumn of 1942 (which is as far as he takes us) is in its own way equally striking. His tribulations were not at an end. It was only in 1954 that he emerged from the grip of the NKVD, or KGB as it was now called. The fate of his family, his own experiences, the facts which he had learnt in labour camp, left him a determined opponent of what Pasternak calls 'the inhuman power of the lie'.

Khrushchev's Secret Speech of February 1956 foreshadowed the rehabilitation of many of Stalin's Communist victims, but the military leaders were not at first among them. Strong resistance to their rehabilitation seems to have been put up by Voroshilov, who had shared much of the responsibility for their execution, and by Molotov and others. However, in 1957, and particularly after Marshal Zhukov had been promoted to be a full member of the Party Presidium in June 1957, at a time when Molotov and his associates were expelled from the Central Committee, the names of Tukhachevsky, Yakir and the others began to be mentioned with praise in historical works. The fall of Zhukov in October resulted in the temporary cessation of these moves, and the military men went through a period which has been described as their de-rehabilitation. However – and particularly after Voroshilov was himself removed in 1960 and denounced in 1961 – their full and public rehabilitation finally took place.

During this time, Pyotr Yakir was well treated. In a speech to the XXIInd Party Congress in 1961 Khrushchev personally referred to him in a sympathetic fashion. He came for a time under the protection of leading figures in the Army especially concerned to re-establish the reputations of the officers Stalin had shot under faked accusations. Pyotr Yakir was the most prominent and active surviving member of any of their families. He was given a post in the Institute of History. In 1962–3 he toured the country lecturing on his father. In 1963 he was allowed to edit a memorial volume *Army Commander Yakir* in collaboration with Ya. A. Geller. The Khrushchevian de-Stalinisation, in fact, was gathering way, and partial and incomplete though it was, many people, including Yakir, hoped that it would develop further and further. Such, indeed, seems to have been Khrushchev's intention.

Khrushchev's overthrow in 1964 did not lead immediately to a complete reversal of this trend. But over the next couple of years, the hostile references to Stalin grew milder and milder, and then began to turn into a measure of praise, while those he had victimised no longer had their fates referred to. At the same time, state action against dissenting intellectuals, which had been considerably relaxed in the Khrushchev heyday, gradually intensified.

At this point Pyotr Yakir, rehabilitated and in comfortable circumstances, might have felt that he had done and suffered all that could be expected of one man. He has often been told since by the KGB that he was lucky, and all he now needed to do was to forget the past and settle down as, in effect, an accepted member of the priviligentsia.

He has not done so.

Like other Russian intellectuals, he feels that the past cannot simply be forgotten; that until the truth is told, the Soviet present is inevitably corrupted in mind and feelings; that the established order remains founded on a lie. It is this, above all, which has impelled so many Soviet liberals into their position of resistance. If the truth cannot be told, those who believe that it must and should be are forced into a confrontation with the organs of suppression.

The new 're-Stalinisation' was soon illustrated in a *cause célèbre* in which Yakir was professionally involved. The historian A. M. Nekrich, in his book *22 June 1941*, described the outbreak of the Nazi–Soviet war without concealing the responsibility of Stalin for the initial disasters. The book was published in the spring of 1965, but pressure was then brought by the authorities and it was suppressed, after a stormy debate at the Institute of History in which the great majority of members, including Yakir, strongly defended Nekrich's objectivity. In the end, the Institute itself was dissolved.

But the key moment, from which the whole of the present 'Democratic Movement' may be said to date, was the trial of Andrei Sinyavsky and Yuli Daniel in February 1966. It was above all this gross and provocative frame-up which committed Yakir, too, to his new life as a dissident activist. In March 1966 he was one of 18 who protested in writing against the dismissal of an Assistant Professor of Literature, Duvakin, victimised as a witness for the defence in that trial.

In January 1968 he was a signatory of the 'Letter of the 170' protesting against the trial of Alexander Ginzburg and others. He now spoke flatly of 'neo-Stalinism'. In February he signed the 'Open Letter of 12' to the meeting of world Communist leaders. He was summoned to the KGB on 14 February and accused of being the 'chief instigator'. He spoke at the memorial meeting for the liberal writer Kosterin in November, an occasion on which all the leaders of the Russian, Tatar, and other dissident groups assembled. In fact, whenever protests were made, Yakir's name was now prominent. Russia's leading Christian resister, A. E. Levitin, he defended as strongly as he did the Tatar leader Ilya Gabai.

In March 1969 Yakir wrote a letter which became a classic of the dissident literature. Addressed to the editor of the official party organ *Kommunist*, with a copy to the Central Committee of the Party, it protested at articles which had been appearing in praise of Stalin. (Roy Medvedev, author of *Let History Judge*, recently published here, was provoked by the same pro-Stalin campaign into a similar letter.) The two letters were central in the resistance to the attempt then being made totally to rehabilitate Stalin. Yakir was able to point out that what was now being said – and often by the same people – contradicted the line taken a few years previously. He quoted several of the present leaders, such as President Podgorny, Mikhail Suslow and Alexander Shelepin, with the strong attacks on Stalin they had made as recently as five years ago. The bulk of Yakir's letter, however, was dramatically cast into the form of demanding a posthumous trial for Stalin – which, he pointed out, should be as legal as the posthumous rehabilitations which had taken place. He put forward charges under various articles of the penal code under which, he concluded, Stalin had earned a minimum of four death sentences and sixty-eight years' strict imprisonment – that is, if only a single case in each category were taken into account, whereas, in fact, there were hundreds of thousands of them. In the letter, Yakir quoted in detail, in some cases for the first time, various murders ordered by, suicides provoked by, genocidal acts by the old dictator, including the executions of the wives of prominent military men and the imprisonment and execution of their children, together with Stalin's personal responsibility for ordering the use of torture.

In 1969, too, he and others formed the Action Group for the Defence of Human Rights in the USSR. Its first action was a letter addressed to the United Nations Commission on Human Rights, which the UN office in Moscow refused to accept on the grounds that it was not qualified to deal with private persons. The Group has been active in the whole sphere of Soviet civic malpractices, and half-a-dozen of its members have been arrested, including the poetess Natalia Gorbanevskaya. Yakir was prominent in its work, and also performed touching acts of solidarity, as when he visited Pavel Litvinov in his exile near Tungokochen in Siberia in 1969.

Signs began to accumulate that the KGB regarded him as a key figure. In the summer of 1968 the radio technician, Genrikh Altunyan, until lately an instructor at a military academy with the rank of major, had been expelled from the Party and the Army simply for 'links with Yakir and Grigorenko'. In the summer of 1969, during the interrogation of a civilian they believed to be linked in some way with the group of Baltic Fleet officers then under arrest for forming a society for political democracy, the KGB asked 'Are you acquainted with Yakir?' and told the suspect that they knew that Yakir had put Gavrilov (the leading arrested officer, later sentenced to six years) in touch with him.

The campaign against him also resulted in various unpleasant letters, such as one in the autumn of 1969 from the chairman of the Executive Committee of the town of Sumy, in the northeast Ukraine, who, writing 'On behalf of all the inhabitants of the town of Sumy', said that Yakir had 'chosen the road of betrayal of the interests of the fatherland'. Others wrote that he was 'giving the West food for malicious progaganda'.

Yakir's answer was:

If we are afraid of causing a stir in the West, then we ought once and for all to renounce all criticism, self-criticism and open discussion, to renounce argument; for it is through argument, as you know, that the truth is born. My father, like many other honourable and innocent Soviet citizens, was destroyed by Stalinism. And it is Stalinism I too am fighting against. Do you suggest that in doing this I am bringing shame on the name of my father? Unfortunately there is a tendency nowadays to confuse anti-Stalinism with anti-Sovietism. In this way Stalinism is equated with Soviet power, and this conflicts with the spirit of the 20th and 22nd Party Congresses and the resolutions they passed.

For in spite of the resistance not only of activists like Yakir, but also of a number of major established figures in the literary and scientific world, the neo-Stalinism he noted was making steady progress. There were even voices favouring full reversion to Stalinist falsifications, as when a KGB witness at the trial of Altunyan in July 1969 actually stated in court that it was not yet certain that the rehabilitation of Army Commander Ion Yakir had been justified.

Arrests of dissidents became ever more numerous, and measures to prevent protest got progressively tighter. It had become traditional for protesters to try to make some sort of demonstration in Pushkin Square on 5 December, Soviet Constitution Day. For it is widely felt that if the provisions of the Soviet Constitution were really put into effect, the present repressions would be illegal. On 5 December 1971, the KGB took special precautions, and told those they detained that this was the last time any such demonstration would be allowed at all – previously fifty or sixty people would converge on the square, stand in silence for a while, and then disperse, an act hard to prove illegal even under the new Soviet laws. This time the KGB shadowed Yakir all day and several times warned him not to go to the square. *The Times* (7 December 1971) reports that two KGB men accosted him at a bus stop and said, 'Hello, Petya (a familiar form of Pyotr). So everyone around you has been arrested and you are still sitting at home, torturing yourself.' After attempting, with his wife and daughter, to take part in the demonstration, he was seized and taken to a police station. There he was asked by a KGB official why he continued to protest. 'Let us talk man to man. Why did you have to go there today? What is your need? Are you not happy in your work?' Yakir replied that he had been banned from working as a historian, upon which the KGB man said that they could put that right. Yakir then said that his daughter had been expelled from her Institute, and the official again said that this could be reversed. In fact every inducement was offered to him to recant. But he was also warned that he should cease 'public activities' and told by the interrogators, 'You aren't your father's spiritual heir! We are his spiritual heirs!'

Pyotr Yakir, and others of his family, have been much harrassed. But the KGB has not, or has not yet, felt it possible to go further. Yakir is still to some extent protected by his father's name and his own reputation: to rearrest him, as has been done with Amalrik, Bukovsky and scores of others, would be so flat a declaration of re-Stalinisation that the political leadership has not so far found it expedient to do so. A remark to Yakir by the KGB official before whom he was brought on 5 December 1971 shows something of their attitude. He said 'Which way do your eyes face? Forwards or backwards? You're always looking backwards. We understand, of course. You have had a hard time. But you ought to look to the future. Everything's fine.'

There seem to be two elements in the reluctance of the leadership, as yet, to go to extremes. First, while they reject any real repudiation of the Stalin heritage, they do not now want a re-enactment of the Stalin terror: apart from anything else, they are hardly likely to forget that it found its highest proportion of victims among the Communist leadership itself. Then again (as has been shown on earlier occasions) the arrest or persecution of leading liberal activists brings protest from much wider circles. A complete suppression of such activities as those of Pyotr Yakir would be a signal to Party and society alike that Stalinism proper, even if not yet in its most bloodthirsty form, had fully re-established itself. Nor should it be quite excluded that there are still elements in the top leadership ready to play the anti-Stalinist card in any power struggle.

Nevertheless, these are precarious safeguards. And as I write there are sinister signs of further moves against the libertarian element. In mid-January 1972 Yakir's own apartment was searched, and many documents were seized, while similar moves were made against other liberals. At the same time, the press has been carrying calls for the further tightening of ideological discipline and vigilance.

Yakir, who is married to Valentina Savenkova, has had the full support of his family. His daughter Irina was a student at the Institute of Historical Archives. There she was expelled from the Komsomol in the autumn of 1968, for having stood outside the courtroom during the trial of Pavel Litvinov and others on 9 October, for their Red Square demonstration on 25 August against the invasion of Czechoslovakia. In 1969 she was several times reported in minor trouble, for example being present when a friend's flat was raided in Kharkov; she was detained briefly on 6 June, and then expelled from the Institute. On 20 August 1969 she was one of the signatories of a protest on the anniversary of the Czechoslovak invasion. She continues with these activities to this day, being one of the signatories of an appeal (of which her father was one of the sponsors) to the Secretary-General of the United Nations on the Bukovsky Case in January 1972.

Pyotr Yakir was intending to write the rest of his life story. He has lately been ill, and it is doubtful if he has been able to produce any more: if so, it has not yet reached the West. Meanwhile, neither illness nor persecution have shaken him, and he faces both with the assurance that, in his own words, 'The ideas proclaimed have begun to spread widely throughout the country – and that is the beginning of an irreversible process of self-liberation.'

Postscript

As this book goes to press, we have the news of Pyotr Yakir's arrest, on 21 June 1972. As I write, he is reported in the Lefortovo prison and is believed to be facing charges of various types of anti-Soviet activity. In fact, the fears expressed in this Introduction seem to have been realised. We must hope – and in the interests not only of Yakir himself, but of progress and liberty in the USSR, and in the long run in the interests of world peace and understanding as well – that better counsels may have prevailed and that he may have been released by the time this book appears. Meanwhile, the message he recorded for the West some months ago has now been published (in *The Times*, 23 June 1972). In it he tells us that if he 'confesses' it will be the result of torture: 'You will know it will not be the real me'; and that if he is reported as committing suicide, it will in fact be murder. He tells of how he was recently urged by the KGB to give up his activities, and how he replied 'There is nothing we would like better than to give it up. But you keep handing out twelve-year sentences to people.' He concludes:

'Well, all you people in England, I greet you, however much you do or do not help us.'

A Childhood in Prison
by
Pyotr Yakir

I
My Father's Arrest: Astrakhan

It was 30 May 1937; the day before, my father and I had been at the dacha in Svyatoshino, outside Kiev. The telephone had rung. It was for my father. Voroshilov[1] was on the line.

'Set off for Moscow straight away, for a meeting of the Military Council.'

It was past midday. My father replied that there would be no more trains for Moscow that day. He requested permission to travel by plane.

'Don't bother. Take the first train tomorrow.'

The train for Moscow next day left at a quarter past three. I went with my father to see him off. He was very uneasy. He knew that in the last few weeks a number of high-ranking military officers had been arrested, including Mikhail Nikolayevich Tukhachevsky.

My father's words of farewell to me were: 'Be true to yourself, son!'

When the train moved off, I noticed several men in NKVD uniform boarding the next to the last carriage (the saloon carriage in which my father was travelling was the last one).

When I got home to our flat in Kiev[2] I asked my mother's permission to go out (I had two more exams to take before the

---

[1] Kliment Voroshilov, People's Commissar for Defence, was one of Stalin's leading accomplices in the purge of the Army. After Stalin's death he became Head of State but was removed from all posts in 1960–1. After Khrushchev fell he was reinstated as a member of the Central Committee.

[2] The Yakirs, like most privileged Soviet families, had a flat in town and a dacha in the country.

end of the school year); she told me to be back before ten o'clock in the evening.

At ten o'clock I said goodbye to my friends in the Mariinsky Park opposite our house. The policeman, who was always on guard outside our house, said nothing to me. I noticed that the lights were on and the blinds drawn in every room in our flat. I rang the doorbell. For some time no one came to answer it, and then a man's voice asked: 'Who's that?'

I said that it was I.

'Oh, Petya,' the voice said, 'the thing is your mother's had a heart attack and the doctors are with her. You stay out for a bit longer.'

I dashed off back to the park. When I got there, some Serbian women began pestering me to let them tell my fortune; some of my friends were standing round when the fortune-teller said: 'You will never see your father again. You have a long long time in a state building ahead of you. Everything will turn out all right for you in the end. You'll have a wife and two children.'

I came back home at about one o'clock in the morning. The lights were still burning in the windows of the flat. The door was opened, when I rang and I saw two men in NKVD uniform. One of them told me fairly sharply to go into my father's study. There at the desk sat a big man with a broken nose. He was in NKVD uniform, with the badges of a Commissar of the Second Rank (I found out later that it was Yezhov's deputy, Frinovsky, one of the most notorious interrogators in the NKVD at that time).[1]

'You've taken your time,' he said. 'Well, you can tell us now where you keep all that foreign currency.'

'In the first place, I've no idea what's going on here, and in the second place, I know nothing about any foreign currency.'

He rose quickly from the desk, strode over to me and struck me on the head, apparently not with his hand, but with some object, as the blow was a heavy one. I fell.

---

[1] Mikhail Frinovsky was, as Yakir says, one of the worst of the NKVD chiefs. He was eventually appointed People's Commissar for the Navy, and was executed some time in 1939.

'Take the little puppy away,' he said.

I was dragged to my feet and taken into the dining-room, where my mother lay on the sofa. She had had a heart attack. She kept on asking for coffee. She was not alone in the flat. Some friends of the family, Sergei Ivanovich Sapronov, President of the Ukrainian Communist Party Central Committee Medical Commission and his wife, Vera Alexandrovna Komerstein, the editor and pilot, had also been detained during the search.[1]

Mother could not give me a coherent account of what had happened. The search continued. About twenty NKVD men were involved. They tapped all the walls, took up the parquet floor and dug up parts of the garden. They didn't leave till lunch-time on the following day. They took away sixty-four weapons, for the most part weapons that had been presented to my father (there were gold and silver swords, various kinds of rifles, pistols and even experimental submachine-guns – the 'Dyegtyaryovsky' and others). They also took some large-scale maps with the measurements in versts,[2] lists of military personnel from the Kiev Military Region, who were at that time serving in Spain – but left other documents, including private letters.

Frinovsky himself gave no explanations. One of his men said: 'Don't get excited. Everything will be cleared up.'

By the next day I had realised the significance of what had happened. I then set about removing from the flat anything that might arouse curiosity (models of tanks, aeroplanes and ships, which had been given to my father, his pipes, etc.) and giving them away to my friends. In the park I met Ira Peterson

[1] They were arrested later that same summer: he died in the Kolyma, and she served eight years in the camps and died after being released. Their son, a boy of eleven called Yura, lived alone in their flat for several days after they had been arrested. Each day he would go to the NKVD enquiry windows and ask where his mother and father were. Afterwards he was sent to an orphanage. When he was sixteen he joined the army and was wounded several times; he now lives near Moscow. *Author's note.*
[2] A Russian measurement, now no longer in use, equal to about two-thirds of a mile.

whose father,[1] a former Kremlin Commandant, had been arrested a month before mine. After her father's arrest, she hadn't wanted to talk to me, but now she dashed up and said:
'You and I are in the same boat now. . . .'

My mother telephoned the First Secretary of the Central Committee of the Ukraine, Stanislav Vikentievich Kossior,[2] and asked him to have us moved to another flat. He said that he would send a man who would take care of everything. Days passed, but we stayed on.

On 7 June the NKVD Special Branch sent for my mother. The Branch chief, Kupchik, and his deputy, Shorokh (both recently appointed), spoke to her. They tried to calm her down, telling her that all would be well. They asked her to write my father a note about things at home, in which she was to say that everything was all right and Petya was taking his examinations. Mother wrote the letter. When they had read it, they told her that what she had written would not do. They kept telling her what she could and couldn't write. The letter had been rewritten four times before a text was arrived at which satisfied them.

On 8 June, she was sent for a second time, but this time for a different purpose. She was informed that a decision had been made to exile our family and we were offered a choice of three cities: Aktyubinsk, Akmolinsk or Astrakhan.

My mother chose Astrakhan, whereupon we were told to leave within forty-eight hours. My mother stated that she could not be ready in such a short period. She was told: 'You'll have to be.' That very same day some people turned up and began to pack our things.

---

[1] A. A. Peterson had been removed from his post in the Kremlin in 1935 for lack of 'vigilance' and transferred to Kiev. He was arrested there and shot in 1937.
[2] S. V. Kossior, full member of the Politburo, was arrested in April 1938 and executed on 26 February 1939, on charges of connection with 'foreign counter-revolutionary organisations'. His wife was also shot as a 'relative of an enemy of the people' and so were three of his brothers. The fourth, also a member of the Central Committee, committed suicide.

In the afternoon of 11 June, we left Kiev. Some books and certain essential things were packed in wooden crates to be sent on by slow freight: all the furniture, the crockery, the bulk of the books – around 7,000 volumes – were left in the flat. When the family was rehabilitated[1] however, the official inventory of this property was missing.

S. I. Sapronov and all my classmates went with us to the station, but none of our other friends made the decision to come and see us off.

That same day, the central newspapers contained a short report that the Special Office of the Military Collegium of the Supreme Court, under the Chairmanship of Ulrikh[2] and with Budyonny, Blyukher, Shaposhnikov, Belov, Alksnis, Kashirin, Dybenko and Goryachov[3] as assessors, had heard the charges against Tukhachevsky, Yakir, Uborevich, Kork, Eideman, Primakov, Putno and Feldman,[4] who were accused of treason under article 58–1b, 58–6 and 58–11 of the Criminal Code of the USSR. This was all that was contained in the report.

That evening we bought some evening newspapers at a station on the way, which reported that all the accused men had been sentenced to be shot. On the morning of 12 June, after we had arrived in Moscow, we read that the sentence had been carried out.

[1] i.e., in the 1950s.
[2] V. V. Ulrikh, Chairman of the Military Collegium of the Supreme Court, conducted all three of the fake 'Moscow trials' of 1936–8, and many other cases.
[3] Of these, Marshal Blyukher and Army Commanders Belov, Alksnis, Kashirin and Dybenko were later shot, while Corps Commander Goryachov committed suicide.
[4] Marshal Mikhail Tukhachevsky, Deputy People's Commissar for Defence; Army Commander Ion Yakir, commanding Kiev Military District; Army Commander I. P. Uborevich, commanding the Byelorussian Military District; Army Commander A. I. Kork, Head of the Frunze Military Academy; Corps Commander R. P. Eideman, head of the civil defence organisation Osoaviakhim; Corps Commander V. M. Primakov, Deputy Commander, Leningrad Military District; Corps Commander V. K. Putna, Military Attaché in London; Corps Commander B. M. Feldman, head of the Command Staff Administration. For their trial see Appendix 1.

After our ticket had been endorsed, we changed stations, from the Kiev to the Paveletsky. Two hours before the train was due to leave, two men in NKVD uniform came into the waiting-room and invited my mother to accompany them into some kind of office in the station building. They kept her for about an hour and a half. Approximately half an hour before train departure time, she came back to us, her face all stained with tears. In the train, mother told how they had demanded that she repudiate my father and tried to prove his guilt to her. She refused to repudiate him, but in the train kept on repeating to herself: 'Surely he couldn't. I don't believe it.'

After our arrival in Astrakhan, unbeknown to my mother, *Izvestia* published what purported to be her repudiation of my father. We didn't show her the paper. The next day, however, Uborevich's wife brought it over to us. My mother immediately wrote to the NKVD saying that she intended to protest formally about the publication of a repudiation which she had never made. 'You do that,' they said to her. We persuaded her that it was useless, and the protest was not written.

In Astrakhan we stayed at a hostel for new arrivals and about two weeks passed before we could find a room to rent. Eventually we found somewhere to live. Our housekeeper, Maria Yakovlevna Proshina, left, and my mother's father, Lazar Petrovich Ortenberg, arrived.

The city headquarters of the NKVD withdrew my mother's passport and showed her an order of the Special Board (OSO)[1] under which she was sentenced to five years' administrative exile, as a member of a traitor's family (ChSIR), and given a document, whose reverse side was divided up into sections, which had to be marked off twice monthly on certain days.

[1] The Special Board consisted of the Deputy Head of the NKVD, the Plenipotentiary of the NKVD for the RSFSR, the Head of the Main Administration of Militia and the Head of the Union Republic NKVD where the case had arisen. The Prosecutor-General of the USSR or his deputy was also to participate. It was set up by laws of 10 July and 5 November 1934 and was given 'cases for which the evidence was not sufficient for turning the defendant over to a court'. (*Sovietskoye Gosudarstvo i Pravo* No. 3, 1965.)

At that time the families of Tukhachevsky, Uborevich, Gamarnik,[1] who shot himself on 31 May 1937, Kork, Feldman, and of a number of NKVD officials, who had been arrested, were living in exile in Astrakhan. This last group included the families of Ostrovsky, Nevolik, Steinbruck, Markaryan and Yagoda.[2] There was also Anna Mikhailevna Larina, Bukharin's[3] wife; at that time he had not yet been convicted. (She was the daughter of a well-known Bolshevik, Yuri Larin, who was buried by the Kremlin wall.) Radek's[4] wife, the father of Gai[5] (one time chief of the NKVD Special Branch) and the families of many others were also there.

By this time Astrakhan had indeed become a place of exile. Even by the beginning of the 1930s, a number of people connected with the opposition had been sent there; also some Social Revolutionaries, Mensheviks and anarchists. They were continually being arrested. Moreover, in 1935, after Kirov's murder, about 4,000 families from Leningrad were sent there (they included former members of the nobility, priests, merchants and their families). One might meet a count working as a caretaker. By the time we arrived they had all got used to the situation and worked wherever they could.

For two whole months, none of the newly-exiled persons could find work, since no organisations would take them on. The majority of the exiles had no money and they all lived, as indeed we did, by selling rare books and other valuables. (I

[1] Army Commissar First Class Yan Gamarnik (the only victim of this case not to come to court) was Head of the Army Political Administration.
[2] Genrikh Yagoda, Head of the NKVD until September 1936, was one of the accused in the March 1938 trial and was executed. The others were prominent subordinates of his.
[3] Nikolai Bukharin, arrested at the end of February 1937, was the principal accused in the great trial of March 1938, and was executed.
[4] Karl Radek was one of the leading accused at the January 1937 trial, at which he was sentenced to ten years' imprisonment. He died in a labour camp. His daughter later got eight years.
[5] M. I. Gai had himself conducted many notorious interrogations, including that of Ion Yakir's personal friend, Divisional Commander Dmitry Schmidt.

remember how I myself went to sell the Academy Edition of *The Lay of Igor's Host* with the Palekh illustrations, and got 100 roubles for it.) The ladies from the capital assembled at the NKVD building twice a month to have their papers marked.

The horror that had begun in the country continued. From the newspapers we learned all the time of new arrests and suicides.

My mother exchanged letters with her sister who lived in Sverdlovsk. Her husband, Ilya Ivanovich Garkavy,[1] had been arrested in April 1937, and as it later transpired, had made an end of himself in Lubyanka-2 by smashing his head against the wall. His wife, Emilia Lazarevna, came and joined us with her two children.

On 1 September 1937, we exiled children went to school. On 3 September, however, all the exiled wives, apart from my mother, Nyusya Bukharina (Anna Mikhailovna), Natasha Makaryan and Garkavy's wife, were arrested.

We ourselves were present at the arrest of Uborevich's wife, Nina Vladimirovna. When a search took place, the first thing to be confiscated was private correspondence. A document would be compiled listing everything else. You could take with you as many essential articles[2] as you could carry. As we later learned, the women were dispatched to No. 3 block of Astrakhan prison and the children to the Astrakhan NKVD children's home.

I stopped going to school and spent my time paying illegal visits to the garden of the children's home, cheering up the kids, and taking notes from them to the women's prison, where I made a reasonable job of throwing them across to their mothers during their exercise period.

On 14 September it was our turn. By the time I returned home, there was a pile of things, which had already been given a good going over, lying in the middle of the room. An NKVD

---

[1] Corps Commander Garkavy, commanding the Urals Military District. His death date is given as 1 July 1937.
[2] Toilet requisites, handkerchiefs, socks and other clothing, etc.

senior lieutenant, called Moskovkin, was in charge of the search. I can remember two interesting details of the search itself. The searchers brought to light a book, published in Germany, about the new German army, which had a swastika drawn on its cover. They were quite delighted by this and thought they had uncovered a new Fascist plot. There was also a light-calibre artillery shell I had, which was empty inside and in which I kept my collection of foreign coins. When he spotted it, Moskovkin crept cautiously towards it and picked it up with trembling hands.

'What's this?'

I said: 'Take the top off, and you'll see that the shell's empty.'

He undid it, and a heap of foreign coins in small denominations poured out on to the table.

'Foreign currency!' cried Moskovkin.

It was about eleven o'clock in the evening when mother and I were put on a lorry and taken away. Grandfather and the Garkavy family were left in the house. The Garkavys were picked up a week later.

The lorry with mother and me on board stopped at the women's prison. I spent a long time consoling my mother, who was sobbing, because she did not want to be parted from me. Then she was unceremoniously dragged away from me, bundled into the prison and I was taken on to the children's home, where the kids, who were still not asleep, greeted me with delight. Among the children of my age (12–14) who were there, were Tukhachevsky's daughter, Svetlana, Uborevich's daughter, Mira, Gamarnik's daughter, Veta, Steinbruck's daughter, Gizi, and Feldman's son, Syeva. All the others were younger, including even some three-year-old children.

The older ones were very attentive to the younger ones, trying to take the place of their mothers.

Three days passed, during which I managed to get a name as the ringleader of the 'traitors' children. On more than one occasion, I authoritatively informed the revolting hag who was in charge of the children's home, that children did not answer for their parents, and therefore we should be treated simply as children. There had been cases when our mentors had called the youngsters little vipers and other names.

At about eleven o'clock in the evening of the fourth day, we heard footsteps. I lay on my bed, with half-closed eyes and saw the woman in charge of the home pointing her finger in my direction for the benefit of some man in NKVD uniform. I was got out of bed, told to get dressed and collect my things. All the children came running into our room, demanding to be told where I was being taken. The NKVD man assured them that, as I was the smartest of the lot, I was to be sent first, as he put it, to be given a job in the fish factory at Ikryanoe, where all the others would follow me without delay. The girls were in tears when I went out into the street, where a small van was waiting for us. We drove off, and stopped at the NKVD building. I was taken into the duty room. A few minutes later another man in NKVD uniform walked up to me, and, levelling a revolver at me, shouted: 'Hands up!' I put my hand up, more out of stupidity than anything else: I had no feeling of fear. I was searched carefully, and when they reached the turn-ups of my trousers, I asked venomously: 'Hoping to find a tank there?'

The man who was doing the frisking snarled something in reply, and was highly delighted, when he found in my small suitcase a tiny knife, which my father had given me, with the handle in the shape of a horse's head.

'An offensive weapon!' he shouted.

Then they sat me on a bench, where I stayed for about three hours. I lit up one of my father's pipes, in which I smoked a mixture of tobacco and hemp, given to me by young criminals at the children's home. My head began to spin. I wanted to laugh, everything seemed so improbable. At that very moment some fellow came in and asked: 'Where's Yakir?'

I got up, feeling rather unsteady on my feet. I was taken off to my first interrogation. It was three o'clock in the morning of 19 September 1937.

Before going on to describe the first interrogation, I would like to recall certain facts which the wives of the arrested men recounted while we were living in Astrakhan.

According to what Tukhachevsky's wife, Nina Evgenyevna, told us, on 9 June 1937, an NKVD official came to her flat in Moscow with a note in the handwriting of her husband, Mikhail Nikolayevich. It contained the following message: 'Dearest Ninochka, please bake an apple tart for Ion (my father) and me.' She said that she would bake the tart. On the following day officials came to collect it. It was the day before the trial. Apparently this was the last wish of the accused men.

Why Mikhail Nikolayevich wrote 'Ion and me' remains a mystery, as they were not in the same cell.

Blyuma Savelyevna, the wife of Gamarnik, told us that on the morning of 30 May, Jan Borisovich Gamarnik, who was at home in bed very ill (with severe diabetes), was visited by his deputy Bulin[1] and supposedly by V. K. Blyukher. They informed him of the arrest of Yakir and Uborevich and after talking for a short while, they left. Some little time later the roar of an engine was heard and the doorbell rang. Gamarnik's wife went to answer the door. Jan Borisovich asked the nurse, who was on duty looking after him, to bring something from the other room. Just as the outside door was opened, a shot rang out in Gamarnik's sick-room. The senior NKVD officers at the door pushed Gamarnik's wife aside and rushed into the sick-room, but it was already too late – he was dead. Regardless of this, they cut the telephone wires and at once sealed the safe and the drawers of his desk. A few days later Gamarnik's body was cremated; the only persons present at the cremation were his wife and Yelena Sokolovskaya.[2] The urn with Gamarnik's ashes was placed in a dovecote near the crematorium, but a few

---

[1] A. S. Bulin, candidate member of the Central Committee, arrested and shot later in the year.
[2] Formerly the secretary of the Underground District Party Committee in Odessa during the Intervention of 1918, at that time head of Mosfilm, and wife of the People's Commissar for Agriculture A. Y. Yakovlev [later head of the Agricultural Department of the Central Committee. Shot on 14 March 1939], herself arrested and shot shortly afterwards. *Author's note.*

days later it was removed on someone's orders and disappeared, no one knows where.

I should add that the wives of Tukhachevsky, Uborevich, Gamarnik and Kork, who were sentenced to eight years under the same rubric as we were (member of a traitor's family, ChSIR), were shot in October 1941.

I was taken into a fairly spacious room. At a table sat that same interrogator, Moskovkin, who had come to arrest us at home. In the middle of the room stood a chair, on which I was told to be seated. The man who had brought me remained in the room and kept walking to and fro, sometimes standing behind me. As I was 'high', I found it unpleasant to have him standing behind me. I kept on turning round.

'Stop turning round!' the interrogator shouted.

'Stop him standing behind me. I don't know what he's going to do.'

Moskovkin asked him not to stand behind me.

For some reason or other, I kept on thinking that the interrogator was some kind of great big bourgeois in a top hat, who was sitting a long, long way away from me, just like in the illustration in Alexei Tolstoy's book, *The Hyperboloid of Engineer Garin*.

When he had noted down my personal details, the interrogator read the charges out to me in a monotonous voice: 'You are charged with having organised a band of Anarchist cavalry, whose aim it was to be active behind the lines of the Red Army in the event of war, and also with spreading the Anarchist ideas of Bakunin, Karelin and Kropotkin among schoolchildren.' I stated that I did not know who Bakunin and Karelin were, but I had in fact read the published letters of Kropotkin. A brief altercation between myself and the interrogator then ensued on the question of why my cousin, Yura Garkavy, and I used to cross over to the far side of the Volga and go riding on the horses which were grazing there in the Kalmyk steppes.

'It's just that we love horses, my cousin in particular.'

'We know that you did this for training purposes, in connection with the charges here preferred.'

Apart from this, I was also charged, on the basis of evidence given by one of my girl classmates (I can't remember her name), that I used to tell anti-Soviet jokes. Which ones? That I can't remember either.

Some time later, a big man, with two rhombuses[1] on his colour facings, came into the office. As I learned later this was Lekhem, the chief of the city NKVD.

'Comrade cheif, the little snake won't confess,' Moskovkin said.

'To hell with him,' the chief replied. 'We'll sign the confession ourselves.'

'But what right do you have to sign yourselves?' I shouted.

The lanky fellow walked over to me and said deliberately: 'You're in no position to talk about rights.'

Then he turned to the interrogator and said: 'Finish the thing off.'

The interrogator made a telephone call. A guard came. I was taken downstairs, and in the same duty room, the same man who had brought me from the children's home, said sleepily: 'Well, now we'll go and fix you up with a job.'

We got into the same van and off we went. It was just after five o'clock in the morning when we drove up to Block 3 of Astrakhan prison, which stood by the river Kutum. My escort rang the bell, handed over some kind of paper, and said: 'Here you are.' A man in warder's uniform said quite softly: 'This way.'

I was taken into the duty room. The prison officer in charge was asleep in there. They woke him up.

'They've brought a new lad.'

He asked languidly: 'Convicted or on remand?'

I said 'convicted', because I thought that I'd been given five years' exile at the same time as my mother.

When I'd been searched perfunctorily and an official inventory had been made of all my things, which were then put into store, I picked up my small suitcase and was taken to a door on the ground floor. The door had the number 7 on it. The warder

[1] NKVD Commissar of the Second Rank.

unlocked the cell door and pulled it open with a creak. 'In you go,' he said.

I crossed the threshold and the door closed behind me.

In front of me was quite a large cell with two big windows, covered by iron shields: most of the floor space was taken up by iron bedsteads with mattresses and blankets on them. What struck me most of all, however, was that all the inhabitants of that cell, and there were about forty of them, had long, long beards and long hair. Then from the far end of the cell came a deep bass voice: 'Oh, see what a fine young lad they've sent us! . . . We'll soon have him dancing. . . .'

I was taken aback and remained standing by the door. Someone else said: 'Now why are you frightening the boy. He's only small, can't you see.'

A short man came over to me, took me by the hand, and said: 'Come on, come on. There's nothing to be afraid of.'

He brought me into the centre of the cell and sat me down on a bed. All the others gathered round us. I was a little bit frightened, because they all looked so strange.

'Well, tell us what you've done and where you come from . . .' said the same bass voice.

I began to tell my story. As I later discovered, they were priests – 'Heliodorites'. Heliodor had been Archimandrite of Tsaritsyn and had fled the country during the first years of Soviet power. On several occasions he had sent letters to priests. This was sufficient grounds in 1937, for the arrest of every priest in Astrakhan and Stalingrad, and for them to be declared to be involved in an anti-Soviet organisation linked with the émigré Heliodor. They had all already been sentenced and had been given terms from five to ten years.

In the cell, apart from them, were two Don Cossacks from the village of Uryupinskaya, who had been accused of preparing a Cossack uprising. In fact nothing could have been further from their minds, but they had nevertheless both been sentenced to ten years.

At eight o'clock in the morning rations were brought round. At that time adults got 600 grammes of bread, but I was brought a larger ration, as juveniles were entitled to 800 grammes. I had some sweets in my case. My cell mates fussed around me, giving me a mug of strong tea, a piece of balyk,[1] a piece of pork fat and even a hardboiled egg. I spent the whole day telling them about myself, my mother and my father. They listened with gasps and sighs and said: 'Now what will these sons of anti-Christ get up to next: putting little children in prison for nothing at all.'

In the evening after supper (in the daytime they gave us soup like dishwater, made from a small fish called 'tuk' which had been ground up; it was normally used to make fertiliser. Nobody ate this incidentally, because they all had food parcels of their own) all gathered round the oldest of the priests who was called Father Andrew, and began to sing in low voices. They sang, by the way, not only sacred music, but also such songs as 'Evening bells'[2] and even 'A night for treason'.[3] They had fine voices. The acoustics in the cell were excellent, and the effect was stupendous.

The door of the cell was opened and two warders came and listened to the singing.

At about ten in the evening we all went to bed. I had been given a bed, a mattress and a blanket and so I too lay down, but for a long time could not get to sleep. At last I fell asleep. I dreamed that my father lay in a coffin in the Hall of Columns and that I stood by the coffin with Voroshilov. Suddenly, my father arose from the coffin. Voroshilov and I were scared stiff. In the morning when I woke up, my mattress was soaking wet. My neighbour, an elderly priest, shook his head and said: 'That, my boy, is because your spirit has grown weak. Keep your spirit up, or else you will not survive – you will die. If your spirit is strong, your flesh will be strong also!'

Thus ended my first day. I was fifteen years old.

On the third day, the chief of the block sent for me and bawled his head off at me for deceiving the duty warders by saying that I'd already been convicted.

---

[1] Cured back of sturgeon, or other cartilaginous fish.
[2] Russian folk song.   [3] Old Russian prison song.

'I did not know that I was under investigation,' I answered. 'I know that I have been exiled and assumed that I had been convicted too.'

The block chief told the duty warder to have me transferred at once to an investigation cell. I took my case, said goodbye to the reverend fathers, and was taken up on to the first floor. We stopped at the end of the corridor by cell No. 12. The door was opened and I found myself in a cell which was the same size as cell No. 7 on the ground floor, but in which there were twice as many people. It was difficult to move about the cell: the whole floor was packed with beds.

At that time the system of discipline in that block was very slack. They still had not got round to hanging shields in front of the first floor windows, and from our window one could see the river Kutum, a path along which free men and women walked to work at a net-making factory, and the exercise yard. We were allowed to receive any number of parcels once every ten days. The people in the cell were mixed in both age and type. On the whole they were people of the 'second category', i.e. not senior staff. In many cases their investigation, which was over, had been conducted in the NKVD remand prison (DPZ). The DPZ[1] was later known as the internal prison.

One of the prisoners was a workman, who had been convicted under Article 58–7 (wrecking). He and his comrades had stolen wire from the factory where they worked and made nails from it, which they then sold. By this time common or garden theft had begun to be classified as a political crime.

There was one young man in that cell whose name was Kashkin. Before he was arrested he had worked in a packing factory in Astrakhan. It so happened that one night he had been left in charge of the factory. That very night a fire broke out. He was arrested and given three years. This happened in 1936. His parents hired a good lawyer who managed to get the sentence reduced to two years, and then lodged a complaint through the supervisory section of the Procuracy. The complaint was found to be legitimate and a re-trial took place, at

[1] Dom predvaritelnovo zaklyucheniya.

which the sentence was reduced to one year. The parents made a further application to the Supreme Court of the USSR, which revoked the sentence and referred it for further investigation. Time passed, and the new year of 1937 dawned. But then, all at once, the re-investigation was conducted under Article 58-9 (sabotage), and instead of the desired freedom, he got ten years in the camps, without the right of appeal.

All the prisoners in our cell had undergone a new type of investigation. The interrogators had been rough; they had shouted at the accused, intimidated them and sometimes even beat them. As a rule the investigation did not last very long. Some people confessed, others didn't, though in none of the cases had there been corpus delicti. The ones who confessed were referred to the special collegium of the Regional Court, and they at least saw their judges; those who denied their guilt were processed either by the OSO, or the Special 'Troika'. These were extrajudicial bodies which tried prisoners in absentia and sentenced them under headings such as: ChSIR, which I've mentioned earlier, ASA (Anti-Soviet agitation), KRD (counter-revolutionary activity) with the addition of the letter 'T' or 'B' indicating that the subject was either a 'Trotskyite' or a 'Bukharinite', SOE (socially dangerous element), PSh (complicity in espionage), PD (complicity in sabotage), KRA (counter-revolutionary agitation). Ordinary criminals were tried under the heading SVE (socially harmful element).

The terms of imprisonment given by the OSO and the Special Troika were for the most part identical: about 80% of those sentenced got from 8 to 10 years, about 15% got 5 years and the remaining 5% or so were given 3 years.

The only person in our cell who had been connected in the past with the opposition was Ivan Kolotilov. He had belonged to a Trotskyite student group in Moscow, and after 1928 had been exiled more than once. When he was arrested in Astrakhan, a long time was spent trying to make him confess that in 1932 he had organised a group of young people in the town and propounded the idea among them that it was impossible to build communism in one country. When he signed under Article 206 (corresponding to Article 201 in the present-day Code of Criminal Procedure, i.e. at the end of the investigation), Kolotilov, tore open the waist band of his underpants and pulled out a document proving that in 1932 he had been in Semipalatinsk, and not in Astrakhan at all. The interrogator lost his temper, struck Kolotilov on the face and shouted out: 'We'll sentence you in any case!'

Kolotilov's case was destined for the Special Collegium, and that was where it went. After being sentenced, Kolotilov landed in a different cell, right underneath us. With the help of a parachute[1] made from thread, we got from him the story of his trial and were in correspondence with him until he received the answer to his appeal. According to what he said, the court calmly 'digested' the proof that at that period he hadn't been in Astrakhan and sentenced him to ten years' imprisonment. Kolotilov submitted an appeal, in which he stated that never in his life had he spoken of the impossibility of building communism in one country, as he thought it quite impossible to build socialism at all. The court of appeal calmly confirmed the sentence, without paying any attention to this highly criminal statement.

There was also a Jew in our cell called Abram Khaikin. He had lived at one time with his parents in Poland and had been arrested on a charge of espionage. The authorities were trying to elicit a confession from him that he used to go fishing in order to count the steamers going up and down the Volga, and sent this information to the Polish intelligence service. The investigation had taken rather a long time and in December 1937, Abram had been sentenced to fifteen years by a Military Collegium.

The twentieth anniversary of the October Revolution was drawing near. Recalling that for the tenth anniversary a full-scale amnesty had been declared, no one had any doubt that there would be an amnesty this time too.

At the beginning of November 1937 I heard a familiar voice

---

[1] Prison slang for a means of transmitting messages by lowering, hoisting or swinging them with the use of cotton thread or wool.

from the exercise yard. I pushed my way to the window and saw that one of the people out taking exercise was my cousin Yura. I called out to him: 'How on earth and when did you get here?'

'They pulled mother in early this morning, took Volodya[1] to the children's home and brought me straight here to the prison.'

He had not been interrogated, nor had any charges been preferred against him, but since he was wearing military uniform (this was something he liked to do), he was put in a cell with other military personnel. The warders shouted to us to stop talking to one another, but I already knew which cell he was in.

The next morning I took up a position near the window, waiting to see my cousin taking exercise, and was very surprised when I suddenly spotted yet another of my contemporaries, Sasha Agapov, the son of a senior administrator from the Caucasus, whom we had got to know during our exile. I was highly delighted. He turned out to be more talkative than my cousin. He had been arrested on the evening of the preceding day, his mother had been taken to the women's prison and he had gone to be interrogated by Moskovkin. The interrogation had concerned his involvement in our 'band of Anarchist cavalry'. So it seemed that the whole band was where it belonged, i.e. in prison.

On the morning of 7 November, we all put on our glad rags in honour of the October holiday. After lunch someone struck up the *Internationale* which made everybody feel better. Almost everyone in the cell joined in the National Anthem.[2] Somebody got carried away, and pulling off a red vest he was wearing, forced his way to the window, and began waving it through the bars. Suddenly two shots rang out from one of the watchtowers. The singing stopped at once and everyone turned on the person who had been waving the vest, reproaching him for

[1] Volodya Garkavy, Yura's younger brother.
[2] At this time the *Internationale* was still the official Soviet national anthem.

breaking the prison rules. A few minutes later the cell door opened and the warders who had come running up demanded the flag waver to come out into the corridor. He went out. Some time later they came for his things, The warder told us that he had been put in the cooler for fifteen days.

Everyone was impatiently awaiting for 9 November, thinking that that would be the day when the decree of amnesty would be announced.

I was the first one to be allowed to see my relatives, on the morning of the 9th. My friends instructed me to ask detailed questions about what was being printed in the newspapers.

My meeting with my grandfather took place in the presence of a warder. I asked Grandfather whether he had seen the papers. He told me he hadn't, but the food he had brought me was wrapped up in newspapers he had bought that very day.

Before the Revolution my grandfather had been a teacher at the Petersburg Conservatory. After the Revolution he had lived in Warsaw, where he had been a member of a quartet with whom he had travelled round the world. In 1926, after writing to my mother, he came to the USSR. Initially he lived in Odessa with other relations; after 1935 with us in Kiev. He was the only one of the people among whom I grew up who had no qualms about criticising the existing order and leadership of the country. When I asked him whether he had heard anything about an amnesty, he replied, within the warder's hearing: 'Whatever's put that into your head? Surely you don't think the Bolsheviks would ever do anything good?'

He told me that of all the people who had been exiled in 1937, the only ones who hadn't been arrested were himself, Radek's pregnant daughter Sonia, Nina Vladimirovna Uborevich's nephew Slava, and Mashenka, Uborevich's maid. He said that they were getting on well with one another and taking parcels to everybody, that Mother was still in Astrakhan and that he had been several times to the NKVD to request them to set me free. All that had happened, however, was that they had detained his second daughter, Emilia, and his other grandson, Yura. He asked me not to share the dainties he had brought me and said finally that he still had hopes of my being set free. I asked him to give Mother my love, if he was allowed to see her. We kissed one another and, muttering something to himself, he made for the door.

I was taken back to my cell where everyone plied me with questions. I told them that my grandfather knew nothing, but that I had got the latest newspapers. We began to read the newspapers. And – oh horror! – instead of the long-awaited amnesty the front page of the newspaper was adorned by an ordinance of the All-Union Central Executive Committee increasing the maximum penalty under Article 58–1, 2, 6, 7, 8, and 9 from ten to twenty-five years. On page 4 of the paper it was briefly reported that on the basis of this ordinance, two men had already been sentenced to twenty-five years for spying for the Germans. Spirits in the cell dropped at once. One of the prisoners went off into hysterics. The remainder simply made gestures of resignation and tried to prove that the ordinance and the amnesty were quite separate issues and there would still be an amnesty.

After lunch I was sent for and taken downstairs. In one of the rooms stood a camera on a wooden tripod; I was told to sit down on a chair and was photographed in both profile and full face. Then I had my fingerprints taken in another room. The block chief informed me that on the basis of a directive from the people in charge of the city NKVD I was to be transferred to a cell for juveniles. I was taken back upstairs, where I picked up my things, and was taken to the other side of the corridor. When we came to a door with the number 21 on it, the warder said to me: 'Just see that nobody takes advantage of you.'

Meanwhile on the other side of the door I could hear shouts, laughter and swearing. The warder opened the door, followed me into the cell and addressing the persons within, said sternly: 'And don't get the idea you can do him any harm. If you lay a finger on him I'll have you all in the punishment block.'

The kids in the cell were, with one exception, all smaller than I was. The taller one, known as Ivan the Priest, was top dog in the cell. All but two of them were in prison for petty theft. These two, whose nicknames were Abanya and Mashka, had been charged under Article 58–8 (terrorism). They were from an orphanage and were both eleven years old. They had been given a special medical examination to establish spuriously that they were thirteen years old which made it possible to arrest them. They and three other lads from the same kind of background had set fire to the house of the warden of the orphanage in Astrakhan, a man whom they loathed. The warden had not in fact died in the fire, but had sustained burns. Proceedings were instituted, and they were accused of terrorism.

Left alone with my new cell mates, I suggested they help me dispose of my grandfather's parcel. They accepted the invitation as a matter of course. In half an hour the parcel was gone.

By evening it became clear that Sasha Agapov had been moved into the cell for juveniles next door but Yura was still with his soldiers.

The night passed without disturbance. In the morning the bread ration was brought round. Some of the boys gave their ration to Ivan the Priest. He stacked the bread together and began calmly to eat his own ration. The ones who had handed over their rations sat sadly, making sidelong glances at those who were eating. Abanya happened to be sitting near me so I asked him if he wanted a bite.

He nodded. I broke off half and gave it to him. He began to chew frenziedly, but Ivan the Priest turned to me and said: 'Don't give any to those rats. Going without bread won't finish them off.'

As I learned later, the ones who had handed over their bread had simply lost it playing cards. When they saw that I had a copy of Pil'nyak's[1] *OK* the kids asked me whether I needed it. I said that I didn't as I had already read it.

'Oh, that's fine! We'll make ourselves a pack of cards then.'

I gave them the book. They were delighted with the fine shiny

---

[1] Boris Pil'nyak, one of the Soviet Union's leading authors and former President of the All Russian Union of Writers, was shot in 1938 or 1939 as a Japanese spy.

paper – and the 'factory' went into production. Everybody was involved in the work. Some made paste from bread: they crumbled some bread into a mug, mixed it up with water into a sort of modge. Two of them then held a tightly stretched handkerchief, while a third used a wooden spoon to press this modge through the material and on the other side of the handkerchief a milky-coloured paste was formed. Others were involved in cutting out stencils with a home-made knife, burning part of a rubber galosh and producing some magnificent soot, grinding up a piece of red crayon, pulling the book apart and tearing up each page into four equal-sized pieces. After that, they stuck all the pieces together in pairs and put them to dry. When everything was dry and a count was taken, it turned out that eight packs of cards could be made from this book. Their excitement knew no bounds.

After placing the cards together in piles of fifty-two, Ivan the Priest, who was the major card-making specialist, clamped each pack in turn down to the floor with a board and rather deftly cut all the edges straight, before handing them to other lads, who dexterously applied and printed in either black or red, the previously prepared stencils. The result was almost as good as real playing cards.

When the cards were ready, some of the packs were quickly hidden in the damper up near the ceiling, in case there should be a search. The remaining packs were put into use; people sat down to play, having stationed one boy at the spyhole to block it with his body in the event of a warder looking through.

They played mainly two games: Bura or 31, and Stoss.[1]

I was surprised by the simplicity of morals in the cell. No one was embarrassed when someone went to use the slop pail, and towards evening one character began to masturbate quite openly. I was very surprised. There has to be a first time for everything however.

When we were taken out to the lavatory, I left notes there for Yura and Sasha. A few days later I spotted my grandfather

[1] Two gambling games. Bura is akin to pontoon, the aim being to get as near as possible to 31 without 'busting'.

and the pregnant Sonia Radek on the far side of the fence by the river. We were about a hundred metres away from them. I began to wave, but they did not notice me. The lads then suggested the following solution: I should write a note containing all my wishes, then roll it up tightly inside a ball of soggy bread and, without thrusting my hand beyond the bars, throw it so that it flew out between them. My first throw was successful. Grandfather picked up the ball, unfolded the note, and let me know that all was understood.

As the majority of the kids were either from orphanages or from out of town, no one came to visit them and they received nothing from the outside. They asked me to write a special note at once, asking Grandfather to buy some 'plan'[1] and two little 'snakes' (fine saws to saw through the bars). They said they would tell me how these things could be got to us when they were all to hand. I explained these things in my next epistle. which I got to Grandfather by the same method. Grandfather understood everything, and he and Sonia came to hand in a parcel for me.

Conversation in the cell was chiefly about who had stolen what and when, and the fun they had had on the proceeds. The details were recounted with considerable imagination and, of course, embellished. The stories very often involved drinking and girls. I couldn't believe that such small boys were capable of sexual relations. But I was mistaken. One of the kids had hung on to his bread ration until evening when he asked Mashka, who had had nothing to eat all day, 'Do you want a bite?'

'Yes,' Mashka replied.

'Then take your trousers down.'

It took place in a corner, into which it was difficult to see from the spyhole, but in full view of everybody in the cell. It surprised no one and I too pretended not to be surprised by it. There were many other instances while I was in that cell; it was always the same boys who played the passive partner. They were treated like pariahs, were not allowed to drink from the

[1] A narcotic made from hemp, smoked with tobacco.

common cup, and were the objects of other humiliations. Sometimes a kind of race would be held; several boys would begin to masturbate at the same time, and on the following day the losers had to give the winner a lump of sugar each.

My cell mates were never at a loss for new ideas; a favourite trick was to slip a strip of papers between a boy's fingers while he was asleep and set fire to it. When the paper began to burn his hand, the lad would wake up and start to wave his arms about. This was known as the 'balalaika'. They did the same thing with people's feet and called it the 'bicycle'.

They amused themselves in this way when not playing cards. Sometimes they asked me to tell them what were known as prison multi-instalment 'novels'; for subjects I drew on the books I had read.

We were in contact with the cell below us. We sent down our 'parachute' and retrieved it with money attached, which we used to buy five kopek bread rolls from the prison shop. These we dispatched to the other cell which was occupied by political offenders still under investigation, who were not allowed to use the prison shop.

Two days after I had made contact with my grandfather, he, Sonia and Slava, Nina Vladimirovna Uborevich's nephew, turned up at precisely the same place and gave us to understand that they had carried out our commission. When we came out to the exercise yard, they managed to throw something over the fence. The warder noticed what was going on and chased us back into the cell, so that he could confiscate it. He did not manage to do this. Back in the cell, we saw that they had thrown us about forty 'bashes' of 'plan'.[1] From Grandfather's gestures we gathered that they had not thrown over all they had brought. Sasha Agapov and his cell mates were taking exercise by then. We told them to pick up the next lot. This time the operation went off very smoothly and the warder noticed nothing. Four saw blades were thrown over to them. We left a note in the lavatory for Sasha Agapov and his mates demand-

[1] A 'bash' is a small lump of 'plan', about the size of a pea, enough for one cigarette.

ing that they hand the saws over to us. They told us that they would only hand them over after they had sawn through their bars. For the next three days we were biting our nails. They were sawing through the bars right next to us, but we could do nothing but wait. All we could dream of was escaping. Eventually, when we went to the lavatory one evening, we got a note from our neighbours saying that they were quite ready and asking us to make a din in our cell at about ten o'clock that night in order to draw the attention of the corridor duty warder. We were furious with them but could not refuse to help. At ten o'clock we staged a noisy fight: not only the corridor duty warder but the duty officer came running to see what was going on. They were afraid to enter the cell and just knocked on the door and told us to stop. When the din in our cell was at its height, we heard a shot, and several of us rushed over to the window, while the rest continued making a din. We could see nothing from the windows as the fence was poorly illuminated, but we could hear people scrambling down the wall. After the first shot there were three more, followed by complete silence. We found out later that everybody in the neighbouring cell, thirteen people in all, had fled; twelve young thieves and Sasha.

Two days later all twelve of the thieves were recaptured, but Sasha, despite the fact that he'd been wounded in the leg, disappeared. Six months afterwards he turned up at the Nizhne-Isetsk Boarding School,[1] not far from Sverdlovsk, where all the children of the Astrakhan exiles, who by this time had already been sentenced, were living. He was apprehended during his second visit to the school and sentenced to eight years. Later on he was with Yura Garkavy in a camp near Syktyvkar. What happened to him after that I don't know.

The next time Grandfather and Slava threw us some 'plan' was shortly before the New Year. We did not smoke it at once but saved it until New Year's Eve. Then we had a drag or two which we washed down with sweetened hot water and began to bawl out songs. The old underworld song 'Oh the slums of Petersburg' was rendered particularly loudly. The warders

[1] Not a corrective institution.

came running up, but we barricaded the doors with beds and went on yelling. Some of the neighbouring cells gave us mild support. At about one o'clock in the morning, the fire brigade was called out. They turned a hose on us which quietened us down. After that we were all tied up separately. In the morning, on the prison governor's instructions, four of us (Ivan the Priest, Abanya and Kolyunchik and myself) were dispatched to Block 1 of the Astrakhan prison for thirty days in the punishment block.

Block 1 was a huge three-storey prison with walls of massive thickness, probably built some 250 years ago. The punishment block was in a semi-basement and its shape reminded one of a stone chest. At the four corners of the prison building stood four towers, each of which contained three round-ended cells and a short corridor.

Rations in the punishment block were 300 grammes of bread a day and a ladle of skilly once every three days. Our cell was very cold and we were stripped to our underwear. We weren't taken to the lavatory; provision was made to take out the slop bucket and empty it. We were hungry and we shivered with cold, and wailed doleful underworld songs.

While we were in the 'chest' we scratched on the wall with a broken bit of nail the prison slogan:

> *Who hasn't been here is going to get it*
> *And the one who has won't bloody forget it.*

The inscription was cut deep into the wall. On 31 January, when we should have been released from the punishment cell, the prison duty officer who came into the cell asked us: 'Who did that?'

We refused to answer. So we stayed in the punishment cell for a further sixteen days. Throughout these sixteen days we beat on the door and made a din. During those same days we made up this song:

> *Ding dong ding*
> *The little bells chime.*

In style we'll see the New Year in.
Let them punish us till they're silly!
Even keep us without our skilly
We'll be out ere the New Year's gone.

On 15 February 1938, we were let out of the punishment cell and taken back to Number 3 Block. We weren't taken on a lorry, as was usually the case, but in a Black Maria. When we got back we were split up; I alone was taken back to the same cell from which I'd gone to the punishment block. They opened the door and let me in. In there, however, instead of the young thieves were some lads I didn't know at all, with the exception of my cousin Yura Garkavy. Before I had even had time to make the acquaintance of them all they sat me down to give me something to eat; a large bowl of pea soup had been kept for me and a double bread ration. They had known since early morning that I was coming. I ate ravenously, began to feel extremely unwell, and even lost consciousness. When I came to I was in the hospital. I was told I might have a twisted bowel, but three days later I was back in the same cell.

Five of my new cell mates were the children of exiles from Leningrad who, when they were arrested, had been pupils in the ninth class.[1] They had been imprisoned under Article 58–10 and 11 for allegedly forming some kind of monarchist organisation.

Apart from them there was also a 13-year-old Kalmyk boy who, during the first elections to the Supreme Soviet in December 1937, had fired his catapult at a portrait of Stalin. He had been charged under Article 58–8, but with the application of Article 19[2] (terroristic intentions).

By the middle of January, all the juveniles who had been imprisoned under the political articles had been put together,

---

[1] Approximately 16 years old.
[2] Article 19 of the Criminal Code (or its present-day equivalent, Article 18) is applied when there is evidence of the intention to commit a crime, but the crime itself has not been carried to completion.

deprived of parcels and of the use of the prison shop – the regulations were becoming harsher.

Once we had got to know one another, we formed a commune which was named 'Pluto'. A code of rules was compiled and hidden in the same damper where the cards had been hidden earlier. The bread was divided into three portions one for each of the day's meals, and doled out equally. We took turns to have a crust or the middle part of the loaf. Sugar was kept for five days, when a feast would be arranged, which involved burning the sugar and smoking strong makhorka[1] as we ate it. Having organised ourselves into an egalitarian commune, we quickly came to the conclusion that a hunger strike should be declared in defence of our rights. So one morning we refused to take any food and set forth our demands as follows:

1. That we should be permitted to receive parcels and to use the prison shop.
2. That we should be allowed to send for the interrogators to have our cases explained to us.

After we had issued this statement, the duty warder and the block chief came running up every few minutes. At first they tried to use persuasion, then they began to shout and threaten us.[2] Towards evening on the first day, the prison governor arrived and began shouting: 'We'll have you wretches in court! What are you on about? Have you got something against the authorities? Aren't you getting enough kasha? Isn't the boiling water hot enough for you? I'll show you which side your bread's buttered!'

We were unmoved. The next morning when we were brought our bread ration, we refused to accept it. Apart from water nothing passed our lips. Forty-eight hours passed without anyone coming to call. The hunger strike was going perfectly. I

[1] Makhorka is a kind of coarse tobacco made from the stalks of the tobacco plant.
[2] At that time it was considered an anti-Soviet act for political prisoners to go on hunger strike, and adults were afraid to do this. *Author's note.*

argued with my cousin, who said that everything that was being done was right and proper. It was right and proper that we should be in prison. Our parents had been rightly and properly arrested and shot, and Stalin was a genius. I was against what was happening and saw the root of the evil in the sadist who was sitting on the throne.

On the fourth day everyone began to grow weak. To help keep all their spirits up I danced the 'Tsyganochka'[1] in one of my father's shirts, which came down to my knees. At lunch time on that same day the door to the cell opened and a group of bigwigs came in. The duty warder, the block chief, the prison governor and a man in civilian clothes who introduced himself as the city procurator. The procurator did the talking. He asked us to repeat our demands. We repeated them. He replied that the interrogators would come to see us without delay, that we could use the prison shop, but as far as parcels were concerned there was nothing he could do, as they had been instructed in a circular from Moscow that persons under investigation were not to have parcels.

I was the spokesman for the cell in these talks. I said that we would not call off the hunger strike, because Moscow could not have forbidden parcels to juvenile prisoners, and eventually Moscow would have to deal with people who had no respect for the law.

'All right, go ahead, starve yourselves to death,' the prison governor erupted.

They left. On the following day the block chief came to see us and said that our demands had been accepted. Our relations had already been informed and would bring parcels that very day. The interrogators would come on the following day. We all shouted hooray together and told them to fetch today's rations for us. They brought us bread, sugar and kasha. Bearing in mind my bitter experience we began to eat slowly and in small amounts, allowing half an hour to elapse between each session. In the afternoon everyone got a parcel. They contained every imaginable kind of food: clear soup, chicken, duck, sweet

[1] 'The Gipsy girl', a Russian folk dance.

stuff and of course something to smoke. Once again we saw Grandfather, Slava and the other lads' relations, standing together in a group waving to us and we, plastering ourselves to the window, waved back to them. We threw over to them a couple of notes inside some bread, in which we explained everything that had happened. Grandfather made it clear that he had asked for a meeting, but had been refused.

By evening we were already feeling more or less ourselves again, and a day later we were ordered to collect our things together and were transferred to the main prison. We were all put in cell No. 30, on the first floor, which was the same sort of 'chest' as the punishment cell I had been in. The thickness of the wall in the window opening was 2 metres 20 centimetres. There was room for three people to lie down on the window sill; we called this place 'paradise'. The beds, all standing next to one another, were known as the 'earth', and the place beneath the beds was known as 'hell'. My cousin voluntarily spent most of his time in 'hell', whither he would crawl and practise self-torture. He would, for example, stick a piece of glass into his arm, or carve a cross on his chest, and so forth.

That same day we were summoned to see the interrogators and we signed the document officially ending the investigation. There was nothing in any of our files apart from the record of the one initial interrogation. In answer to my question: 'Where is Interrogator Moskovkin then?' the new interrogator answered: 'That's not my business.'

I learned later that Moskovkin and Lekhem had been arrested; the former landed in the same batch of prisoners as two air force pilots whom he had previously interrogated, and they killed him in the Syzran Transit Prison by twice driving a pointed stake up his rectum.

Time passed. Once a week we were herded out into the corridor at night and the cell and our persons were carefully searched. They used to confiscate all sorts of things, even socks and knitted garments because they could be unravelled and plaited into lines.[1]

[1] i.e. for sending 'parachutes'.

At that time we were fed very badly; we were given soup made from rotten maggot-ridden cabbage and tuk.

Opposite us, in a 'chest' which was identical to ours, was a Social Revolutionary[1] from Central Asia whose surname was Albert. He had been in prison since 1922, only occasionally being sent into exile. By that time he had notched up ten years in prison.

The majority of the cells on the second floor were occupied by prisoners serving their sentences. Albert lowered books down on a string and sent us his notes on the history of our country, descriptions of certain episodes in his life and his commentaries on current events. It was from him that we learned that in the autumn of 1937 a further trial had taken place, at which Rudzutak, Karakhan, Kabakov[2] and others had been convicted. At this time, however, he kept us informed about Bukharin's trial, which was then taking place. He did not doubt for a moment that all the accused persons' confessions had been fabricated from beginning to end. We all believed him, with the exception of my cousin Yura. Often after we had been in correspondence with Albert heated arguments would flare up in our cell. Even now, not all the kids had grasped what was happening in the country, but I and many of the others were already well aware of all the lies and treachery which accompanied the mass arrests. Albert told us who occupied the cells on

[1] The Social Revolutionary Party, militant but anti-Bolshevik, had won an overwhelming majority in Russia's only free elections, in November 1917. Its leaders were sentenced to death, but the sentences were suspended, in 1922. They all eventually perished in the 1930s and 1940s. The circumstances are unknown: but there is said to have been a secret 'trial' in 1937.
[2] The trial, held in secret but publicly announced, in which L. M. Karakhan (formerly Deputy People's Commissar for Foreign Affairs) and others were sentenced to death, took place on 16 December 1937. I. D. Kabakov, First Secretary of the Sverdlovsk Provincial Committee, was shot on a charge of leading a 'Urals Uprising Staff'. Yan Rudzutak, formerly full member of the Politburo, was arrested in April 1937, and executed after a twenty-minute secret trial on 28 July 1938. Yakir's informant seems to have confused these cases: but they were all interlocked, and all three men were named as fellow-conspirators in the Bukharin trial of March 1938.

either side of him. They included SRs, Mensheviks and anarchists. They were allowed to have newspapers in their cells. They argued with one another and they too had a sort of peculiar inter-party commune. Albert was transferred into a solitary cell because he had headed the fight against irregularities in the running of the prison (he had been something like the elders in days gone by). He was the first person in prison who instilled faith in the future into me.

Late one night at the end of March, we heard a din on the second floor and the light suddenly became very dim. At that moment somebody sent us down a 'parachute' with a note containing the following message. 'I think our time has come. Goodbye my children. Cell No. 45 has barricaded itself in and is resisting. It's my belief they're going to take us away and finish us off.' We wrote an answer and were going to tie it on to the string, but at that moment we heard a shout from the cell that the note had come from: 'What are you doing?' Then all fell silent, but we could still hear shouting and noise from the other cells on the second floor. We rushed to the door and to the window and began to hammer on the shield[1] of the window and on the door. The racket and hammering could be heard from the other cells as well. A short while later the whole prison was rumbling with a frightful roar of anger. We heard the occasional cry, but by this time they came from the courtyard. Then came the roar of engines.

Some three hours later all fell silent. All this time, despite the disturbance, no one came to our cell.

The next day we learned from the criminal prisoner who doled out the skilly, that all the serving prisoners – ninety-six men – had been taken off and shot on instructions from Moscow. Tradition has it that in Astrakhan people are shot on Parbuchy Hill, on the outskirts of the town.

One day when he was on his rounds, the prison governor took exception to some rude reply of mine and ordered me to be given five days in the punishment block. There were several adults in the punishment cell who had been imprisoned under

[1] These are also called the 'muzzle' or the 'visor'. *Author's note.*

Article 58.[1] Among them was the deputy director of the Caspian Fish Corporation. He lay on the ground, his trousers ripped open along the seams and his legs in bandages. He had been through four-and-a-half days on the 'stand'. The 'stand' was a refined version of the 'conveyor belt'. The 'conveyor belt' consists of an uninterrupted interrogation lasting for several days with the interrogators working in shifts. In the case of the 'stand' the subject has to remain standing all the time and when he can no longer support himself he is held under the armpits by two guards. These methods of interrogation were in constant use at that period. Before losing consciousness, he felt something go in his leg. It was in fact a vein which had burst. His legs were swollen like lumps of wood and his trousers had had to be cut up and used as bandages. He was in a half-demented state and raved all the time in delirium: 'I'm not guilty, not guilty, citizen interrogator.'

A couple of days later when he was a little more himself, he told us that the whole management of the corporation, some eighty or so people, was involved in his case, and that they were accused of wrecking. The majority of them had confessed to the false charges under torture. A few, including him, had held their ground. To be more accurate, they were no longer holding their ground, but were dying as a result of the torture. He told us how quite recently the secretary of the Astrakhan City Komsomol Committee, Nosalevsky, had leapt from the window of the interrogation room next to his and smashed himself up on the street below.

Nosalevsky's story, which might be entitled 'He came clean' went as follows:

'Come clean! Get it all off your chest!'

'I know nothing, I'm an honest Communist.'

'Come clean, Nosalevsky, there's no use trying to deny it.'

'Citizen Moskovkin, I've told you I'm as innocent as a new-born babe.'

[1] Article 58 of the Criminal Code consisted of fourteen sections, covering all types of 'counter-revolutionary crimes'. See Appendix 2.

'Come clean, or it'll be all the worse for you. It's nine days since you had a wink of sleep, you've worn out four of us and you're tormenting yourself. And all to no purpose.'

'I've nothing to come clean about. For the last three years I've been working as First Secretary of the Astrakhan City Komsomol Committee. Ask anybody.'

'We did ask and it didn't do you much good. All the evidence shows that you're an out and out Trotskyite. If you want to lie down, come clean. You've got nothing to say? I could do with a sleep too, it's almost morning. Come clean!'

Moskovkin dozed off and at that very moment, up jumped Nosalevsky, grabbed a marble paperweight, and hit him on the head with all his might. Then he dived straight out of the fifth floor window.

The first tramcar stopped in front of his body, which was splattered on the road. It was the morning of 15 September 1937.

Another inmate of my punishment cell at that time was an engineer from a large building organisation which was planning the building of a roadstead somewhere on the Caspian Sea. Almost all their staff had been arrested and the engineer had been tortured by having his ears burnt with matches and his fingers broken. He had already confessed to the alleged charges of wrecking, which he said he had done on instructions from an unknown agent of Japanese intelligence. After giving evidence against himself, against many of his co-defendants and also against people who had not yet been arrested, he decided to revoke his testimony and asked for the interrogator to be summoned. The interrogator had not come and he had been hammering on the door of the cell, which was why he'd been put in the punishment block. He had a lost look about him and talked to everybody as though he were asking for their forgiveness.

Also in the punishment cell was a military man who had come back from camp for further investigation. In December 1937 he'd been given twenty-five years on a charge of treason. His treason amounted to the fact that he'd been friendly with a divisional commander, who in his turn had known my father well. So it seemed he had been part of a 'traitorous organisation'. He had been tried by the Military Collegium. The court hearings were conducted as follows. Twenty-four hours before the court was due to sit, the accused was put into solitary, where he was given a copy of the indictment. On the following day he was taken into a room in which the three men who had come from Moscow were sitting. The chairman ascertained the correctness of certain personal details, then asked: 'Do you plead guilty?' How he answered was irrelevant. The man was then taken away and brought back again a minute or two later. The court stood up and the sentence was pronounced. Witnesses were not present at hearings of the Military Collegium. Their testimony was simply added to the file of the case. By and large all sentences of the Military Collegium were death sentences, which were carried out without delay. Immediately after the sentence was pronounced, the prisoner was taken straight to some yard or basement and shot there and then. Two or three vehicles stood by with their engines running to cover the sound of the shots. Under this system about 120 men could be convicted in a working day.

The Military Collegium visited regional centres once a month for three or four days at a time. The necessary number of cases was prepared for the Collegium's arrival. Only about twenty per cent of the accused received terms of imprisonment, usually between fifteen and twenty years; the remainder were shot.

From the soldier's story we learned of a new kind of torture. In keeping with the methods of Deputy People's Commissar Frinovsky – that same Frinovsky who had conducted the search at our flat in Kiev – he had been roasted over electric fires. As evidence of this the soldier removed his shirt and trousers and we saw on his back and bottom the awful traces of the burns. After sentence, he had ended up in Prorvlag, which got its name from the island of Prorva in the Caspian Sea, not far from the town of Guriev. The work in the camp was fishing and fish processing. The work was heavy, but one could at least eat one's fill of fish. Two air force friends of his, one of whom had returned from Spain and been awarded the Order of Lenin just before he was arrested, did their fishing from a small motor vessel. On one occasion, when a small storm blew up, they steered their vessel, with four other prisoners on board in a southerly direction, away from the guards' launches. Firing broke out, but the wind was so strong that the skilful helmsmen steered the boat out of view of the camp guards. The frontier guards tried to intercept them, but they slipped safely across into Persian waters. After this incident, all prisoners sentenced under Article 58 were taken off work which involved going out to sea, and the soldier in our story was put in the central camp prison and accused of complicity in the escape. Being unable to find any way of increasing his term (he had been in prison for less than a year out of twenty-five), they sent him to Astrakhan prison, where he insistently demanded to be sent to another camp. This was why he had got ten days in the punishment block.

Life in the punishment block went on undisturbed, but every day there were new stories. Until then I had spent my imprisonment entirely with juveniles, and consequently I soaked up everything the adults told me like a sponge. For me, these five days were a very important time. I had already learned a lot from Albert, but here I saw with my own eyes men who had undergone torture, and listened to their stories. When I got back to the cell I told this to the kids. They were outraged, and my cousin Yura had nothing to say. A few days later I suggested to everyone that we go on hunger strike and demand that we should either be convicted or set free. It was after all already nearly eight months since our arrest without investigation or trial. The only person to support me in this venture was Yura. He and I decided to go on a Japanese hunger strike, i.e. we would not even have anything to drink. We laid in a supply of makhorka and matches, which we hid in the lining of our boots. The next morning we asked for paper on which to make a statement and wrote that we would not take any more food. An hour later they came to fetch us. We said goodbye to the kids and we were escorted down into the semi-basement, which is where the prisoners under sentence of death were kept. It was a corridor of ten small cells, partitioned off from the rest by a double wall of bars. In the cell there were two wooden trestle beds on which we disposed ourselves. The first day the prison governor came to see us and shouted that it was nothing to do with him whether people were convicted or set free, and that if we persisted in our stubbornness then we would probably end our days there.

The next day the Procurator put in an appearance, the same one who had come on the first occasion. He asked us to call off our hunger strike and promised to get an answer to our question. To manage without both food and water is very difficult. Your mouth gets dry, your lips crack. We tried to conserve our energy by not moving about the cell and lying down most of the time.

The neighbouring cells were occupied. Several times we heard people being taken out at night, probably to be shot. We could also hear some kind of movement and sounds of groaning. Any contact with our neighbours was ruled out, because in the death cells there were three extra warders on duty, who kept the cells under constant watch. Into one of the cells they brought three youths, who had been sentenced to death for rape and murder. They shouted and swore; by this time we were past caring. During the first four days we shook some of our makhorka from our boot linings and when we had had a drag or two lay down for a rest. One felt dizzier than after smoking 'plan' and every day we got worse, but not once did the thought of calling off the hunger strike enter our heads. On the fourth day, apart from the prison governor, who came every day, the prison doctor, an attractive young woman, started to pay us a daily visit. She would check our pulse and make us open our mouths.

On the eighth day, Yura lost consciousness and was taken away on a stretcher. I was left on my own. All kinds of thoughts forced themselves upon me. I had already given myself up for dead. It was ages since I had passed water. The last time I had done so the drops of urine were tinged with blood. On the eleventh day I lost consciousness. When I came to I was in bed, and standing near me were two nurses, the doctor and the prison governor. The words seemed to come from a long way away: 'Well, are you going to call off your hunger strike?'

I somehow managed to shake my head.

Yura was nowhere to be seen. He was apparently in some other ward of the prison hospital. They began to feed me forcibly. I was incapable of resistance. They gave me alimentary enemas, fed me clear soup through my nose and gave me intravenous injections of glucose. I felt better and better with each passing day.

On the eighteenth day the prison governor came into the ward with some other person, and held up in front of me a half-sheet of paper divided into two sections. Above was written: 'Decision of the OSO (Special Board) of the USSR NKVD.' In the left hand column it said: 'The charges have been heard against P. I. Yakir', in the right hand column: 'It has been decided to sentence the said person as a SOE (socially dangerous element) to five years in a corrective labour colony.' Below was a signature in red ink, then the word 'chairman'.

My request had been granted. I had been convicted.

'Well, are you going to have some food now?' the governor asked.

I nodded my head affirmatively.

I was in the hospital for about another week and then I was transferred to a cell for adults who had been convicted. On the following day Yura was brought there too. He looked worse than I did. We were both still weak.

There were about a hundred people in the cell. During the two days that we were there two Persians in our cell committed suicide, and in the whole prison about ten others did the same thing. The cause of the suicides was as follows: one fine day, on instructions from Moscow, every person of Persian origin in Astrakhan was arrested. They belonged to two categories: the first was those who had lived in Russia before the Revolution, the other was those who in 1929 after the uprising against Reza Shah had fled from Persia to the USSR. There was scarcely even the pretence of an investigation, and they all received the decision of the OSO (Special Board) on the same day. The ones who had lived in Russia before the Revolution were given ten years each and the ones who had fled to the USSR in 1929 were to be forcibly deported back to Persia, which for them meant that they would be executed once they got home. They would willingly have spent ten years in prison in the USSR, whereas the other group, instead of ten years' imprisonment, would have preferred to go to Persia. The cruelty, however, had been well thought out and the ones who didn't want their heads cut off in Persia did away with themselves in a Soviet prison.

Every day somebody or other was summoned for transfer, and two days later our turn came too.

That morning, Yura and I had a meeting with Grandfather. He looked older than when we had last seen him. He begged us not to go on hunger strike again. In the afternoon we were taken out into the exercise yard, where we were carefully searched. We were then sent to the bath-house and afterwards loaded into a Black Maria and taken to the station. When we were being escorted towards the Stolypin carriage,[1] we caught sight of Grandfather on the platform, sadly waving to us. Inside the Stolypin, fifteen of us were pushed into each compartment. The train moved off. A new period in my experiences had begun – the transit stage.

[1] The name of Peter Stolypin, the great Tsarist counter-revolutionary reformer, was given to the penal railway wagons though, as a recent Soviet writer says, 'Why were these appalling narrow penal wagons called Stolypin trucks? They were of quite recent origin.' (Gurgen Maari in *Voprosy literatury*, November 1964).

2
In Transit

There were only juveniles in our compartment: Abanya, Mashka and two kids who had been accused with them, and sentenced to five years each under article 58-8 by the Special Collegium of the Regional Court. Of the remainder, some were known and some unknown to me and all had been convicted of petty theft under Article 162.

While we were still at the prison we had been searched and then issued with a day's bread ration, a salted herring and two large lumps of sugar.

Fifteen people to a compartment was a very tight squeeze. Only two on the third or top shelf could lie down. The rest fitted themselves in as comfortably as they could in a sitting position. The window was tiny, about the size of a ventilator, with thick glass and a double set of bars. The side of the compartment that opened into the corridor was covered entirely by a narrow-mesh grille. Guards patrolled up and down the corridor all the time. People were let out to go to the lavatory one at a time. We were all watered at one go; they brought a bucket of water; we drank a mug each and it was taken away.

The other compartments contained men and women, packed in the same numbers as we were.

The carriage was an adapted 'Stolypin'. Stolypin himself had had a more conveniently designed type of carriage built. Later I had to use them on more than one occasion. In the original 'Stolypin' a large-mesh grille ran the whole length of the carriage, dividing the escort from the prisoners. The prisoners, however, were all in together and could fraternise with each other. There was a water barrel within the enclosure. Travelling in this kind of carriage was much more interesting and less harsh.

After we had been put in the compartment, the escort commander came up to us with a pile of large envelopes in his hands. These were our personal files. The roll-call, or checking of the 'goods' began; surname, first name, patronymic, article, term.

When he asked me which article, I answered: 'SOE.' He said: 'In future remember that it's not SOE, but 58–10, 11.' The same thing happened with Yura.

We vainly tried to get into a position where we could see what was written on the top of the envelopes. All we managed to do was to read on Abanya's envelope: Nizhnie-Chersk MITK.[1] We had heard of this colony. It was situated somewhere in the Don valley and noted for its severe discipline.

Early in the morning the train arrived at Saratov station. Our carriage was uncoupled and shunted into a siding. After a short while, they began to unlock the compartments and let the prisoners out one by one. 'Get your things and come out one at a time,' shouted the guard. Then we heard the numbers 'One, two, three ... ten ...' echoed by different voices, one after the other in quick succession. First the number was called by the guard who was standing at the door of the compartment, then by the one at the end of the carriage, then by the one at the exit from the carriage. When I emerged from the carriage, there were about twenty men squatting near it on their haunches, in rows of four. I took my place in one of these fours. After everybody had been brought out of the carriage, the escort commander counted the fours, and for the first time in my life, I heard what is known as the 'prayer', which I afterwards had to listen to for years on end: 'Walk in fours, keep together, don't talk, a step either to left or right will be taken as an attempt to escape. The escort will shoot without warning. Is that clear?'

'Clear,' came the ragged response.

'On your feet! Forward!' shouted the escort commander, and the column moved forward.

Apart from the young thieves everybody had got a lot of

[1] MITK – Maloletnyaya Ispravitelno-Trudovaya Koloniya – Juvenile corrective labour colony.

luggage with them and walking was hard work. The fours began to break up and the women demanded that transport should be laid on to move the luggage. The escort commander's shout rang out: 'Halt! Sit down!'

Everyone sat down and the escort commander started to explain in a rather surly manner that there were only another 200 metres to go before we boarded lorries. Everybody shut up. Once again the order rang out: 'On your feet!' and very, very slowly the column moved forward. We were surrounded by an escort of about fifteen men with rifles at the ready and two dogs with their handlers. Sure enough, we shortly rounded a fence on the far side of which three lorries were standing. About thirty of us were loaded on to each lorry and a guard stationed himself at each corner of the vehicle. The lorries set off. We made a short journey through what seemed to be main streets. The town was full of greenery and people were in summer clothes. When we drove up to the prison, which was obscured by trees, we were ordered to get down from the vehicles and form fours. We were squatting on our haunches for about half an hour; sitting was forbidden, even on one's suitcases. Then the prison duty officer emerged with a pile of our files. The escort commander stood beside him. The duty officer called us out one at a time. The same questions, the same answers. When your name was called you got up and went through a narrow door on to the prison premises. There, a little to one side, stood twenty warders, who searched the new arrivals. The women were taken away somewhere into the depths of the prison. We were searched on the spot outside. For a mercy it was warm, as we were stripped and given a thorough going over, i.e. they peered into every orifice and fingered every seam.

After we had been searched we were taken to the bath-house, washed and roasted.[1] We juveniles were then taken to a separate place.

Saratov prison occupies a vast area. There are three three-storey blocks standing quite a long way apart. The main one,

---

[1] Roasting: a procedure of heating clothing in order to rid it of vermin.

Number 1 Block, is a tremendously long five-storey building. We were taken to Block 2 and formed up outside one of the doors on the ground floor. The lock was unfastened and we trooped into the cell.

The cell was bursting at the seams. There must have been about a hundred people in it. They had spread themselves out all over the floor, as there were neither iron nor plank beds. The only clear area was a small piece of floor space around the slop tank. Among us there were 'honest'[1] thieves, who knew that they were privileged people in prison and did not have to sit or sleep near the slop tank. One of our young thieves started to make his way over towards the window. The question was rapped out: 'Hey, where've you come from, squirt?'

'Astrakhan.'

'Do you know Cross-Eyed Borka then?'

'Sure, we've done jobs together.'

'Come on then, come on over.'

While we were picking our way across we could hear shouts from over by the window: 'Come on, mates, move over. Can't you see there are some new chaps.'

'OK. OK. There's room for everybody.'

When we got over to the window there was already enough room for us to spread out our things. We were received by Kostya Korzuby, a twenty-five-year-old Saratov thief. Mashka, being a 'pedik',[2] was placed rather nearer to the slop pail. Certain other persons were segregated from their mates because of their inferior underworld status. The rest were left where they were. When Kostya found out what my surname was he said: 'That's interesting. Did your old man take the name Yakir on purpose then? You know what it means if it's decoded?' And without waiting for an answer went on to explain: 'I am a counter-revolutionary and a traitor.'[3]

[1] Respected and respectable members of the criminal fraternity, observing its code of ethics and refusing to collaborate with the prison authorities.
[2] Pedik (diminutive form for pederast – abusive word for homosexual in Russian.)
[3] YA Kontra revoliutsioner, Izmennik Rodiny.

I was astonished at such an interpretation of my name, but Kostya told me that it was a story he'd heard long ago.

Then they produced a huge piece of pork fat, a handful of sugar and some bread. We ate together and that was the extent of our introductions.

Ninety per cent of the people in the cell had been convicted under Article 58. There were a few rogues and ordinary criminals. Most of the '58s' were Don Cossacks, convicted for 'preparing to stage a kulak revolt'; officials of the Grain Procurement Agency accused of 'wrecking' – they were said to have poisoned the grain; employees of the Raizo[1] accused of 'spreading infectious diseases among livestock'. There were also agronomists, book-keepers and a few doctors, all of whom had been convicted under Article 58–10.

In that cell there was also a Saratov architect. He had been charged under Article 58–9 and sentenced to twenty-five years by the Military Collegium. Under torture he had signed a confession that he and his co-accused, of whom there were more than forty, had blown up the new Saratov Opera House, which at that time was still not completed.

The architect made magnificent chessmen from bread and played chess for days on end with a doctor who had been convicted because he knew Professor Pletnyov,[2] one of the accused at the Bukharin trial. The doctor had been one of Pletnyov's pupils.

From the stories people were telling I realised that what was happening in Astrakhan was going on all over the country. Everywhere innocent people were being arrested, beaten and

---

[1] Raizo – Raionnoye zemelnoye otdeleniye – District agricultural section.
[2] Professor Dimitry Pletnyov, Russia's leading heart specialist, was in June 1937 at the age of sixty-five framed up by the NKVD on a false charge of sexual assault and sentenced to two years' imprisonment. He was then broken down by further interrogation, and forced in March 1938 to confess to the 'medical murder' of his patient Maxim Gorki, on the orders of the opposition, being sentenced to twenty-five years' imprisonment. He was reported still in camp in his eighties, and dying there in 1953.

made objects of ridicule during their investigation. Even the methods employed were the same: the 'conveyor belt', the 'stand', and so on. People were being tried in absentia or in total disregard of court procedure. The number of people arrested was growing all the time. During recent months two large batches of prisoners a week, each of about a thousand persons, had been leaving Saratov prison (i.e. for the camps) and the same number coming in from the districts of Saratov province, the investigation prisons and the prison trains.

The third and fourth floors of our block contained the death cells. In them were people who had been sentenced by a Military Tribunal or a Special Collegium. As I have already observed, the ones dealt with by the Military Collegium itself were shot without delay.

These cells were packed tight, as many people sat for three to five months awaiting confirmation of their sentences. In some cases execution was replaced by twenty to twenty-five years in the camps, but the rest were shot.

A physicist from Saratov university was transferred to our cell. He was one of a group of people who had spent five months under sentence of death. They were all accused of passing secret scientific information to the Germans. The case was of course phoney, but all pleaded guilty. The physicist told us that his neighbour in the cell, the chairman of a collective farm in Saratov province, had got a parcel of things from home wrapped up in a newspaper, in which it was stated that the physicist and his co-accused had already been executed. For the next five months he didn't have a wink of sleep, as he knew that death sentences were carried out at night. Later, after he had been reprieved, he could not imagine how to write and let his wife know, since she was under the impression that he had already been shot.

The next day Kostya Korzuby suggested that he and I play a few hands of Bura for clouts. Initially he lost ten clouts to me, then a further twenty. He suggested a decider, and won it. I then went on to lose three more games to him. Once again he suggested a decider. By this time I was in the grip of gambling fever and the stake was 200 clouts each per game. We each had our share of luck. When, however, I got to a stage of being 5,000 clouts down, I suggested a decider, and when I lost once again, I owed him 10,000 clouts. At this point Kostya got to his feet and said he had other things to do, but that we would continue playing that evening. Abanya (my chief protector) came up to me and said: 'What on earth have you done now? Cards have cost you your life, just like they did in Astrakhan.'

I forgot to say that while I was mastering the game of Stoss in the juvenile cell at Astrakhan, I lost sixty-seven bread rations. I gave up my ration for seven days and then my debt was cancelled. I was warned never again to lose more than five rations, as a man would either die or be driven by hunger to some base act; in effect such a heavy loss *was* tantamount to losing one's life. I bore all this in mind and never again played for such high stakes in bread. I was not, however, expecting the kind of dirty trick I had to deal with in this instance. I thought playing for clouts was a joke. In actual fact it was far from being a joke.

Towards evening Kostya returned from wandering round the cell and suggested that I settle up with him. I reminded him that he had promised to have another game with me. Kostya replied that he was tired and demanded a settlement. I had no alternative but to stick out my head and he, with great enjoyment, began to strike one glancing blow after another. After twenty clouts, one of the bystanders said that he ought not to hit me in the same place all the time. He agreed with this and began to hit me on various parts of my head. After about a hundred clouts, I was beside myself with pain. My head was a mass of lumps, it rang with each successive clout and every inch of it felt like part of one enormous wound. I begged and besought Kostya to transfer the execution to the following day. He stopped, squatted beside me and said: 'But you must realise that it'll be even more painful tomorrow? Well, what else have you got to pay off the clouts with?'

I offered him all my things, which at this time were not in store but with me in the cell. He looked carefully through both my suitcases and my kit bag and decided that in exchange for the 9,850 clouts he would take everything I had: a fur-lined overcoat, two new suits, one of which had a waistcoat, two pairs of kid boots, a silk-covered quilt and even six fine pairs of women's knickers, which my mother had put in my suitcase by accident. To cut a long story short, everything, including one of the suitcases, was paid over to save me from the unbearable pain of the beating.

The next morning my head was still ringing. My cousin, who had silently observed the previous evening's scene, pulled a pair of boots from his belongings and handed them to me without a word. Of late he hadn't been talking to me about anything to do with politics, since such a flood of impressions had poured down on his stubborn head as was hardly likely to confirm his view that everything the authorities were doing was right.

Every day people were summoned for transfer from our cell and other cells, and new people were brought in. There were certain standard terms of imprisonment. Most of the newcomers had ten years.

One night, Abanya woke me up and said that they had decided to 'wash'[1] the collective farmers. When the whole cell was asleep, a few of the thieves crept quietly towards the bags, which people were using as pillows, and slitting them open, very skilfully removed various items of food. When they gave the sign, I received the 'gifts' of pork fat, butter, sugar, rusks, onion, garlic, makhorka, cigarettes, and stowed them away. About twenty sacks were cleaned out, and they provided more than enough eatables. Yura, who was also awake by now, was sent with another lad to fetch the water barrel. We dissolved a large quantity of sugar in the water in the barrel and added a lot of white rusks. In prison this is called tyurya. Then, after cutting ourselves a large hunk of pork fat each, a gang of about twelve of us sat down round the water barrel, got our spoons and began gulping down the tyurya as we ate the pork fat. No time was lost in emptying a barrel holding two buckets full of

[1] Wash – to take something from someone while he is sleeping at night.

liquid and scoffing as much as we could eat. Then we lit up cigarettes and put a sweet in our mouths. This was considered the height of elegance. Being full of food, we couldn't keep still. We began to horse around. We made a row and people started waking up. The ones who woke up discovered the emptiness of their bags and began to grumble. This caused our leaders no discomfiture, for they felt it was an entirely legitimate act of violence on the part of the 'have nots' against the 'haves'. In answer to the complaints voiced from every corner of the cell it was stated that if the malcontents did not calm down, they might pay with their noses, which could easily be cut off with a razor. The cell grew quiet. There was no sense of common cause and no one wished to be the target of possible unpleasantness.

During this nocturnal robbery, Abanya had stolen from someone, along with their food, a twenty rouble note, and now without even waiting for reveille, suggested to Kostya that they play a few hands of cards for hard cash. Kostya agreed: money was the most valuable commodity of all. They played Stoss. In an hour and a half Abanya had won back from Kostya all the things which I had lost, as well as Kostya's own suit and boots.

The bell rang for reveille and we were let out to go to the lavatory. They let us out in two shifts as there were only twenty squatting places. We went first and when we returned we saw that two men from our cell were standing with the duty warder and pointing our chaps out to him one by one. The warders standing by in the corridor began grabbing hold of us: Kostya Korzuby, Yura and me and the rest. We squealed, scratched and offered resistance, but were nevertheless escorted into the cold, windowless cell next to our own, which served as a punishment cell. My cousin Yura was the major casualty of this resistance; his arm was badly hurt. When the doctor came it transpired that it was broken and it was put in plaster.

Yura was a generally unlucky fellow. While still a child in Leningrad, during a battle between two districts, he was hit in the eye by a stone fired from a catapult, here he got his arm broken, and in the Komi ASSR in 1941 he was almost killed by Estonians to whom he was trying to prove Stalin's infallibility. In 1942 he was set free from prison and, after spending just one day with the young woman he loved, he volunteered for service in the army. He was killed a few months after arriving at the front, on 12 September 1943.

I was given five days in the punishment cell, but in fact was transferred on the first day. All the others stayed behind. Abanya made me take back all my things. Despite our continual ideological arguments, Yura and I kissed one another goodbye. I was sorry to leave him, as he was very helpless and crestfallen. His belief in justice and what was actually happening on the outside could not be reconciled.

We were taken to Block 1, where we climbed right up the fifth floor and above. Stretching the whole length of the block was a vast attic, packed tight with prisoners. There were about 800 men in it. It was the main transit cell and people were taken directly from there for transfer. The whole world was there! Various nationalities – Georgians, Uzbeks, Chechens, Azerbaijanians, Volga Germans, Kalmyks – were represented in large groups.[1] The Russians, the Jews and the Ukrainians wandered in among these groups like floating atoms. The mood in the national groups was one of elation. People talked animatedly among themselves, asked questions about other fellow countrymen, recalled various stories. One might encounter a middle-aged father and his two sons, or a grandfather, a son and a grandson from the same family. There were many such cases among the Caucasians, since whole families had been arrested. To the already familiar charges a new one was added: the charge of bourgeois nationalism. Most people had been given ten years. On the whole they had been dealt with by the OSO and the Special Troika, and hadn't been bothered too much during the investigation; simply arrested and convicted in absentia. As far as I could make out Party members had borne

[1] The Chechens from the North Caucasus, Kalmyks from the steppe west of Astrakhan, and Volga Germans were deported en bloc to Siberia in 1944, 1943, and 1941 respectively.

the brunt of the onslaught, with the intelligentsia in second place.

Everybody had their belongings with them. There wasn't even room to turn round, but the place was very lively, like a huge eastern bazaar. I shall never forget the grandiose prison concert. No sooner had everybody returned from their evening visit to the lavatory than songs were heard from all corners of the attic. At first there were just a few people singing softly, and then one mighty chorus took up the singing of plaintive Georgian songs. Russians and Ukrainians also joined in the concert. The warders of course demanded silence, and the concert ended.

The next day I and several others were sent for and after being put through the bath-house were taken to the gates, searched, brought outside, loaded on to lorries and taken to the station. The carriage in which we were to travel was coupled to the train and we set off. We were travelling for eight hours. We reached our destination at night, and in the morning they began to unload us.

THE FIRST ATTEMPT

The iron mesh door of the Stolypin carriage grated open: 'Out you get!'

The prisoners came out along the corridor in single file. The guards counted us four times in the space of a hundred metres: one counted us as we came out of the compartment, a second at the end of the corridor, a third as we came down from the footboard, and the fourth not far from the carriage where the prisoners were made to sit down in fours. 'Sit down' is precisely what I mean as standing was not allowed.

When the whole carriage had been unloaded, the escort commander intoned the 'prayer': 'No talking as we go, keep together, a step to the right or left will be taken as an attempt to escape, the escort will fire without warning, is that clear?' A chorus of 120 voices answered: 'That is clear.' An escort of ten men armed with two dogs encircled the column. The order rang out: 'On your feet! Forward!' In the middle of the batch were some twenty or so women, whose expensive clothes were quite out of keeping with their worn out faces.

The batch was taken out to the Balashov town transit prison, which was three kilometres from the station. The road was bad, just a sea of mud. The column was already about a kilometre from the station when we came to a crossroads where a lorry was stuck, its wheels skidding wildly. The escort commander, for either interest's or curiosity's sake, gave the order: 'Lie down!' Everybody at once slumped down in the mud. After the order 'On your feet!' which was given some three minutes later, it was amusing to see how awkwardly the women got to their feet, wiping the mud from their expensive clothes as they did so.

A kilometre further on, there was a bazaar on the right. At the front right-hand corner of the column, a tall man, formerly a pilot, coolly dropped his raincoat over the head of the nearest guard. A second later and from the four corners of the column, four men rushed simultaneously in different directions. The escort was taken aback, several shots rang out, and a number of voices shouted: 'Halt! Lie down! Halt!' Suddenly a boy of fifteen rushed out from the centre of the column and darted to one side. He heard shouts and firing, but on he ran, not knowing himself where he was going.

He found himself in a bazaar, tried to dive into the crowd, but landed in the arms of a hefty policeman. Then the guards were striking him with the butts of their rifles, and a dog was tearing at his clothing. He was carted off to the prison with this symphony ringing in his ears. He heard a snatch of conversation: 'Two got away.' His eyes fell on two bodies lying by the gate of the prison. When they had checked his basic details (surname, name, patronymic, date of birth, article, term of imprisonment) they took the boy through into the prison yard. There they struck him again and again, and afterwards when he was scarcely breathing, they carried him to the bath-house and left him alone. He lay on a bench, unable to get to his feet.

All at once a half-naked woman entered the room. She came close.

'Petya!'

'Milya?'

It was his aunt. She too was on her way somewhere. She had already been in there for three weeks, working in the laundry. She bathed the blood from his body. Yura, her son, was still in the prison at Saratov.

Someone was coming. His aunt went away. He was dragged off to a cell, a dungeon, half underground. The weather was blazing hot, 40°C., and in the cell were five Georgians under Article 58.

'Well, never mind,' said one handsome, grey-haired Georgian, 'You'll be fit by the time you get married.'

The cell where I was was in a semi-basement. Next morning I was told that someone wanted to speak to me at the window. I could scarcely move and by the time I got to the window there was no longer anyone there, but I was given half a loaf of stove-baked bread and a piece of pork fat. 'A little woman who went by left this for you.' I realised that it was Aunt Emilia Lazarevna Garkavaya.

A few days later she came again to the window, gave me some sugar and said that she would probably be transferred the following day. That was the last time I saw her. As I learned later, she landed in the BBK (the White Sea-Baltic Camp Complex). At the beginning of the war she was sent with a large batch of women prisoners to a station[1] called Dolinka in the Karaganda camps, where she died in 1945, a month before the end of her sentence. Her younger son, Volodya, who was born in 1928 and after his mother's arrest spent the pre-war period in an orphanage, was killed in action on 23 March 1945.

Such was the fate of the Garkavy family.

My stay in Balashov has stuck in my memory as a lump of pain. In the ten days I spent there I ached so much that I couldn't lie still. I groaned and spat blood. Ten days later I

[1] The camps in the Soviet Union are often known by the name of the nearest railway station, which may well have been built specially to serve the camp.

was again on my way. I reached the transit prison at Syzran. It stands at a railway junction from where lines run to the north, the north-east and the south-west. The building looked very pleasant. Its three freshly whitewashed storeys stood in a rectangle round a courtyard on to which its windows opened. All the cells were the same, designed for about fifteen persons. At that time there were sixty people in each. Every twenty to thirty minutes somebody was sent for transfer and somebody fresh was brought in. Just as in Balashov, everyone there had been convicted under Article 58 and they came from all over the country. We were fed on skilly made from oats, or cabbage soup made from rotten vegetables.

In our cell there were several men dressed in good leather overcoats and riding breeches with leather gussets. I discovered that they were 'KVZhD-men', people who had formerly worked on the KVZhD (Chinese Eastern Railway), which ran across Manchuria. After the railway was sold to Japan by the Soviet Government, they and their families were transferred to the Soviet Union and were settled mostly in the Far East, though some were sent to Central Asia. In 1937, however, most of them were arrested; the senior employees were shot and the remainder sentenced in absentia under the heading PSh, i.e. Article 58–6 espionage; the men to ten years, the women, the old men and the young people to from five to eight years in the camps. This was the second full-scale action of this kind of which I learned (the first being the affair of the Persians). The Chinese Eastern Railway affair involved several tens of thousands of families. They too were not beaten during their investigation, as the simple fact of their connection with the Chinese Eastern Railway was viewed in itself as guilt, requiring no further proof and calling for a specific punishment.

Each new prison gave me yet wider knowledge of what was happening outside.

In Syzran I got to know a Moscow doctor called Sokolovsky, sentenced to fifteen years. He had been accused of links with certain medical circles which were allegedly involved in 'poisoning' Party leaders.

For a short time, a pilot from the Kiev Air Force Brigade, whose name I don't remember, was in our cell. When he discovered who I was, he came over to me and never left me until the moment he was taken away, some two hours later. He had been in Spain and came back from there with Pavel Rychagov,[1] in the spring of 1937. He was decorated with the Order of the Red Banner and then arrested in the autumn of the same year and sentenced to fifteen years for spying on behalf of Germany. He had a very tough investigation. He was beaten, his leg was broken and it was a long time before he grasped what was happening. This man, who had volunteered to go and fight the fascists, been wounded in the arm and shot down nine fascist planes, could not come to terms with having to sign and accept responsibility for a preposterous accusation, and also slander many of the people he had known in Spain. What did it all mean? When the protracted torture was over he was totally demoralised, broken and almost out of his mind.

After the trial he wanted to commit suicide. He cut a vein but this was noticed and he was first bandaged up and then beaten up. He had not the heart to make a second attempt. He was very envious of the chief of the Air Arm of the Far Eastern Forces, [Corps Commander] A. Lapin, who managed to hang himself in his cell. He told me that Air Brigade commanders Zima and Salnikov, who had also been in Spain, had been arrested, as had the commander of the Kiev Air Force Brigade, A. Bakhrushin and the Brigade Commissar S. Nemirovsky. [Corps Commander] F. A. Ingaunis, who had left his post as Air Force chief of the Kiev Military region, and was travelling to replace Lapin in the Far East, was arrested en route and dispatched back to Kiev.

After the pilot left us, I was upset for a long time, for I had met a man who knew people that I knew and who had been able to tell me of the tragic fates that had overtaken them. I had already stopped thinking about myself. As far as my own fate was concerned, the writing was, as the saying goes, on the

[1] Rychagov – a famous Soviet pilot and hero of the Spanish civil war. Later a general, he was shot in October 1941.

wall. When, however, I learned what had been the lot of others, and in particular of the things that had happened to people whom I had regarded as models of heroism, I felt still more sick at heart. I saw the explanation of all this horror in the perfidiousness of Stalin and his henchmen.

I was in Syzran for about two weeks and then it was back into the Stolypin carriage and further on my way to Chelyabinsk Transit Prison. We arrived in Chelyabinsk early in the morning and spent twenty-four hours stuck in an uncoupled carriage. They had issued us with only one day's bread ration, but we had already been in the carriage for more than a day. No move was made either to feed us or to unload us, and in answer to all our demands we were told: 'You'll soon be off the train and then you'll get something to eat!'

After twenty-four hours we were unloaded. It transpired that there were six other Stolypin coaches alongside us. They too were unloaded, then we were all formed up in a single column of about 500 prisoners in all, and with an enormous escort and barking guard dogs, were taken right across the town, straight along one of the main streets from which the traffic had been sealed off. The column was long and it was difficult to keep it together. The front ranks kept on being halted so that the stragglers could be chased up at the rear. We were marched along the roadway and townspeople on the pavements stopped and gazed at the passing procession. Their glances held neither sympathy nor censure. The man beside me was surprised that we were not being taken to the municipal prison, but in fact, as it turned out, this was full up. We had been sitting in the carriages until the construction of some large huts to serve as a temporary transit prison was completed.

Three hours or so later we reached some kind of building with a new fence round it. It took us three more hours to get inside the compound. In it there were three huts, each capable of holding up to a thousand men. One was already packed tight, and the other two stood empty. We were herded through the bath-house, largely for formality's sake as there were no bowls and many of the taps were not working, and all put in the same hut. Feeding us took a further two hours. For my first time in prison the bread I was given contained oat husks. The skilly was made from rotten fish. Hungry as I was I couldn't eat it. Exhausted by the march and the bath-house, I climbed up on to the top shelf of one of the double-tiered plank beds, all there was to sleep on. I would very soon have gone to sleep, but a circle formed close by me in the middle of which sat an old Uzbek with a moustache, performing some kind of ritual.

In front of him he had a pile of beans, as I later discovered there were forty-one of them, and he was telling fortunes, by a method known as 'kumalak'. The pile of beans is first divided into three lots, each of which is again divided into three before the beans are set out. The fortune-telling involved the use of terms like: 'the head is free', 'a stone lies on the heart', 'the legs are bound'. Almost everybody was given precisely this reading. Next morning we were taken to the lavatory; this did duty for an exercise period. As we were herded out into the yard, where a wooden lavatory had been set up, the Uzbek continued his fortune-telling. He said to one of those who wanted his future told: 'Your legs are unbound: you see that there's only one bean down below, which in prison terms means that you'll be called for transfer any time now.' Everybody was amazed, as we had only arrived on the previous day. Five minutes later, however, the doors of the hut opened and the duty warder called this man's name out. When the latter responded, he was told: 'Get your things and be ready to go.' I was immediately intrigued by all this hocus-pocus. I went over to the Uzbek and gave him a packet of makhorka (each person who wanted to know his fate offered the Uzbek something) and asked him to tell my fortune. He spread out the tools of his trade and said to me: 'Your head is not free, there are two stones lying on your heart, but your legs are unbound.' I replied that apparently this time he had guessed wrongly; they could after all hardly summon people for transfer one at a time every five minutes. I was way out, however. Less than three minutes later I too was sent for and told to take my things with me. The magician of course was delighted because his prediction had come true.

In the courtyard with my file in his hand, stood the governor of the transit prison. After twice checking my personal details (surname, name, patronymic, article, term of imprisonment), he asked me: 'Are you the son of the famous Yakir?' I said that I was. 'You're about to be transferred.' I was taken to the guardhouse and then escorted alone in the direction of the town. It was the first time that I had been asked whose son I was, or had sensed any kind of special treatment at all. It was not specially soft treatment, but showed a kind of wariness on the part of the authorities. I thought I was being taken to the station, but in fact I was brought to the main Chelyabinsk prison. I assumed that the batch would be made up of people from the prison, but after being put through the bath-house I was taken to a cell containing convicted prisoners. I had no notion what was behind all this.

There were about 150 inmates. Two men were lying on each bed, two men sitting on each bed head and two men lying underneath each bed. The ones who were sitting and the ones who were lying down changed places with one another every four hours. There wasn't an inch of spare space in the cell and one had to step over people to get to the slop tank. When the skilly was handed out the bowls were passed from hand to hand. The windows were bricked up to three quarters of their height and the remaining strip of light was way out of reach. I stood by the door unsure of where to go next. Suddenly, from the far end of the cell, someone shouted for me to make my way over. The other people were told to let me through, and I gradually picked my way across to the man who had seemed to know me. He was a former officer, whose rank corresponded to the present-day rank of Lieutenant-Colonel; beside him was a Czech engineer and a third person, a professor, whose name I don't remember. They were, so to speak, the cell command. The military man was the elder and the other two were deputy elders. They were surprised that I had been put in that cell, as I was the first case they had known of a juvenile sentenced under Article 58. When they learned who I was, however, they understood why and treated me with great sympathy.

Literally everybody in this cell had been sentenced to death by the Military Collegium and Tribunal. Each of them had spent several months in the death cells before his sentence had been commuted to a long term of imprisonment. Most of them had twenty years, some twenty-five and some fifteen. They were for the most part engineering and technical staff from the Chelyabinsk tractor plant, foreign specialists who had come to work in the Soviet Union, Party workers from the armed forces and also doctors, teachers and others. They had all been tortured while under investigation. The majority had signed the confessions concocted for them by the investigating authorities. They recounted sadly how, unable to withstand the torture, they had confessed to fantastic charges involving both themselves and their friends and relatives. Often the interrogators forced them to sign statements giving grounds for the prosecution of people they didn't even know. Although it was known in the death cells that most of them would be reprieved, no one slept at night. In Chelyabinsk prison there were between twenty and thirty people in the death cells.

One day when our skilly was brought, the door was closed after the skilly server had come into the cell. Previously the door had been kept open while the food was doled out, which let a little fresh air into the cell. On instructions from the elder, the people near the door began to hammer on it and demand that it should be opened. When this was refused, the elder made his way to the door and in accordance with the wishes of the whole cell, sent for the corridor duty warder, and told him that the cell would go on hunger strike. A few minutes later the cell door opened and the prison governor stood before us.

'So you don't want any grub?'

We explained that it was stuffy in the cell and the door was usually left open while the food was being doled out. The governor replied angrily: 'Take the soup pans away!'

They were removed and the door banged to. We continued

to make our indignation felt. After about an hour and a half, three men from the cell were sent for and an hour later I too was summoned. Standing outside the door were two warders who grabbed my arms and took me right across the prison into another wing. There we went down into a semi-basement and entered a room with a table in it. At the table was the prison governor and beside him a man in NKVD uniform. When I was brought in the NKVD man came up very close to me and struck me in the face.

'Come on then, tell us, who instigated this act of counter-revolution?'

'I don't know what you're talking about.' I endeavoured to explain that no one had instigated anything; the conditions in the cell were quite simply unbearable. I was struck a second time, and when this evoked no response, I was dragged into an adjacent room to the sound of the governor shouting: 'The jacket'll loosen his tongue all right.'

In the next room I was thrust into a canvas jacket, which was longer than I was tall and had long sleeves. Then they threw me face downwards on the floor, put my hands behind my back and tied the sleeve ends together. After this they tied these ends to the hem of the jacket and fastened the knot to a rope, which passed through a pulley hanging from the ceiling. Then they began to hoist me upwards in short jerks, kicking me in the ribs as they did so. First of all my body bent and my stomach remained on the ground.[1] The pain was excruciating. When I was pulled clear of the floor, I lost consciousness. They doused me with water and quickly brought me round. The same people were still standing there, but a doctor in a white coat was holding my hand and feeling my pulse. I was again asked whether I was going to talk. Again I told them that I knew nothing. The onlookers swore at me obscenely. The hoisting procedure was repeated twice more, after which the prison governor turned to the NKVD man and said: 'All right, we'd better let them take him off to the punishment block; if he pegs out we might get it in the neck because he's on a special

[1] A common method of interrogation, known as 'the swallow'.

warrant.' (Prisoners travelled on special warrants in particularly important cases.)

I spent five days in the punishment block. All the time I lay there my whole body was racked with pain. The first two days I couldn't even eat my 300 gramme bread ration. On the fifth day I was sent for and could hardly drag myself along. My things had been brought from the cell and were with the duty officer. I was taken out into the yard. The warders brought my things out. They put me in a black maria, and took me alone to the station, where they handed me over to the Stolypin carriage escort commander, whose carriage was already packed to capacity. All the other people in the compartment were on Article 58. Some were travelling from one camp to another. They told me a lot about the camps.

From them I heard stories of the BBK (White Sea-Baltic Camp Complex built up on the basis of the earlier White Sea Canal). There were camps there dating from the beginning of the twenties, such as Parandovo, where the prisoners used to be kept in the forest for a couple of days at a time without being brought back to the camp, until they fulfilled their work quota; Kem, a vast women's camp where they did tailoring work; Shavan and Yuzhny, camps for juveniles; the Third Watershed, where about three thousand Moscow homosexuals were deported after the canal was built; Medvezhia Gora, where the 'wet nurses' were: women with children who had been born in the camps; Segezha, which was where they kept the wives of the enemies of the people; UChPP[1] – a camp where recidivists were held. At the beginning of the twenties these camps were part of USLON,[2] and the steamer that plied between the mainland and the islands was known as the 'elephant'.[3]

We reached Sverdlovsk in the morning. I saw for the first time

---

[1] Probably Uchotnaya Chast Povtornykh Prestuplenii – i.e. Recidivist registry.
[2] Upravleniye Solovetskikh Lagerei Osobovo Naznachenia: Solovki Islands Administration of Special Purpose Camps.
[3] *Slon* in Russian means 'elephant'.

a black maria with the words 'ice-cream' written on the side (later I saw lorries with 'bread', 'meat' and other things written on them).[1] This was done to keep the movement of prisoners secret. The black maria brought us straight into the yard of Sverdlovsk prison. We were unloaded and told to sit down on the ground. While we were waiting for the local authorities to accept us, we took stock of the prison. On one side stood the long three-storey building of the old prison, built in the time of Catherine the Great. The windows had 'shields' over them. A five-storey, red brick block, with large unshielded windows had been built on to it in the shape of a letter C, forming a closed rectangle. This was the transit prison, the old 18th century block was the investigation prison. From what the duty warders said, the transit block had been built in 1936 as an army evacuation hospital, in the event of a war with Japan. Afterwards bars were put on the windows and it became a 'splendid' transit prison, with high ceilings, large windows and, in normal conditions, large cells for sixty or seventy persons. In 1938, however, there were between four and five hundred people in each cell.

They began sending for people one at a time and taking them to cells. I was left on my own. For some reason nobody sent for me, although several times people came up and asked me where I was going, but this was something of which I was entirely ignorant. According to my file envelope, I was to be handed over to the Sverdlovsk Regional Administration of the NKVD – but they were the people who did not know what to do with me. It was Sunday. They brought me a bowl of skilly and a ration of bread. Still I sat in the courtyard, warming myself in the sunshine. Towards evening I was put in a van and driven away. I found myself in the courtyard of a large building; some windows giving on to the courtyard had bars on them. This turned out to be the Sverdlovsk City Internal Prison.[2] I was put in a cell without being searched or having my things

[1] See the last chapter of Alexander Solzhenitsyn's *The First Circle*.
[2] Internal prison. A prison within the walls of the main NKVD building in the town, comparable to the Lubyanka prison in Moscow.

taken from me. It was a 'station', which is the name given to cells in prison where prisoners are held prior to transfer. The cell had plastered walls, which were covered with inscriptions such as the following:

'January 5th '38, from "Voenka"[1] to the firing squad, Bauer, engineer of Uralmash.'[2]

'I shall die a communist,' followed by the date, 'taken to the firing squad.'

'Let my family know at (then followed an address), that I was shot on such and such a date,' followed by a signature.

I was amazed that these inscriptions had not been erased; many of them had been made two or three months before my arrival. There were fresh inscriptions too, made only the day before.

I walked along the walls, reading this ghastly chronicle. I was alone in the cell. The thought that I too was to be shot kept coming into my head. The duty warder opened the door. I asked him what they intended to do with me. He answered calmly that I would spend the night there, and in the morning the people in charge would come and sort things out. Then he gave me a piece of bread, a mug of hot water and some sugar.

This somehow reminded me of home and I did not refuse it. That night I could not get to sleep. I kept thinking of firing squads. I went over my memories of Astrakhan and Chelyabinsk. Exactly the same thing was happening here in Sverdlovsk. Mass executions of completely innocent people had been going on for over a year. What on earth was happening in the country? When people close to the centre of power were wiped out, it was somehow comprehensible – Stalin was consolidating his authority and the people helping him changed like patterns in a kaleidoscope. Today you're an NKVD chief or the newly-appointed secretary of a district Party Committee, tomorrow you're arrested, and the next thing you've been shot. But the imprisonment and execution of run-of-the-mill engineers, doctors and writers was beyond understanding. They,

[1] Abbreviation for the Military Collegium.
[2] Uralsky Mashinostroitelny Zavod – Ural Engineering Works.

after all, were not obstacles on the tyrant's road to deification. Apparently the breakdown of law and order had permeated every level of the state and led to an orgy of blood.

At about eleven o'clock in the morning I was summoned from my cell and taken to the investigation block, to the office of the chief of the Sverdlovsk NKVD. There they spoke to me in a kindly manner, told me not to worry and that my fate would soon be decided. I was taken away, put in a van and driven back to the transit prison, where, after searching me, they put me in cell number 77. According to the roll, there were 563 people in this cell. They were a mixed bunch, by and large 'special settlers' from the Urals and Western Siberia. They had all been convicted in absentia and most of them had been given ten years. The 'special settlers' were the so-called kulaks and their families, who had been deported between 1929 and 1932. Many had died of hunger and cold in the places to which they had been sent. The survivors were being purged and accused of espionage, acts of sabotage, wrecking, and in some cases of preparing an armed uprising.

I volunteered for work in the kitchen and cleaning vacated cells, etc. I managed to get into conversation with other cells, including cells with women in them. One woman told me that a few months previously my mother, Nyusya Bukharina and Natasha Makaryan had passed through Sverdlovsk Transit Prison on their way east, and shortly before my arrival, my father's sister, Isabella Emmanuilovna Belaya-Yakir, had been briefly in their cell. As a prisoner on the service staff, I ate quite well and made some contact with the warders. Sometimes at nights, when the 'birds' from the juvenile cells were washing the floors, some of us were allowed out into the corridor and permitted to spend half an hour with some girl in a separate cell.

Batches of prisoners left the Sverdlovsk Transit prison very frequently, almost every other day, and not in isolated Stolypin carriages, but whole trains at a time. A train of twenty-five to thirty carriages would be made up. All those being transferred would be searched out in the yard, loaded on to lorries and carted off. For half a day at a time the prison yard looked just like a real bazaar.

The cells would be empty. In our cell for example at one stage there were only sixteen people left. That very night we noticed a line of people walking from the investigation block to our own. They were carrying kit bags and suitcases. Ten minutes or so later the door of our cell opened and the duty warder called out loudly and cheerfully: 'Here comes the tram!' (This meant reinforcements.) Then people began filing into our cell in just the same way that the others were crossing the yard. There were about 400 of them. During the ten minutes that they had been on the way from the entrance to our block to the cell itself, there had been time enough to inform them of the OSO decision. They had gone past a small table on the staircase landing, where an NKVD officer had asked their name. When they had given it, he had informed each one that he had been sentenced to ten years in the camps. It was not even suggested that the prisoners sign an acknowledgement that they had been informed of their sentence.

There was an engineer in our cell who told us how three months previously he had been put in solitary and handed an indictment in which he was charged with espionage on behalf of the Japanese. The next day he was brought into an office where three men were sitting (it was a Military Collegium), who asked him his first name, patronymic, surname, etc. When he mentioned his birthplace, the same question was twice repeated, and then they had him taken away. Everything fitted, apart from his birthplace, and he almost got shot by accident.

One evening I was sent for and taken across the courtyard to the office of the prison security officer in the investigation block. He told me to roll up my sleeves. After scrutinising my tattoos, he remarked venomously, 'So you've decided to join the underworld then? You're going to make a run for it? All right, you have a go! Tomorrow you leave for the camp. It's lucky for you I found out you intended to escape, or else you might have been here in this transit prison for a long time yet. But don't you forget. Things might work out for some people, but we'll catch up with you wherever you get to. You're not round the family dinner table now.' (I had been talking in the cell about my wish to escape and apparently someone had squealed.) An hour later I was called for transfer. I was given the usual day's bread ration and a salted herring and carted off to the station. They put me in a Stolypin carriage in a compartment by myself. When the train moved off the escort commander said to me: 'We'll be there in six hours. Don't go to sleep.'

It seemed a very long six hours. Eventually I was told to get my things together. The train stopped and I got out.

3
The Verkhoturie Colony

There were three people waiting for me on the platform in the darkness. A middle-aged man who, it transpired, was Kartashov, the warden of the Verkhoturie Disciplinary Colony for Juveniles; a woman, Lyudmila Sergeevna Anikeeva, a senior counsellor; the third person was a guard. Lyudmila Sergeevna was the product of a commune, i.e. she had been brought up in the Kungur Labour Commune. Before that she had been a thief. Products of the Commune very often worked as counsellors in colonies. But in 1938, at the Bukharin trial, the former chief, of the USSR NKVD, Yagoda, in response to the question of Procurator-General Vyshinsky, 'On whom did you rely?', replied, 'On products of labour communes'. After this statement most former commune members were arrested and sentenced, as traitor's accomplices, to ten years' imprisonment under Article 58.

Pogrebinsky[1], NKVD chief for the Gorky region and founder of the first commune at Sarova, which provided the material for the film *Ticket To Life*, shot himself, because he did not wish to be a party to the arrests. Lyudmila Sergeevna was one of the few people not to be arrested. She told me how real rehabilitation work had been done in our splendid communes at Bolshevo, Kungur, Sarova, and in the Kharkov Communes headed by Makarenko.[2] Almost all her friends were arrested, and she decided to commit herself totally, no longer to the work of rehabilitation, but to helping imprisoned children. She was very sympathetic to me and helped me a great deal.

We set off from the station, right across the town, to a

[1] These rehabilitation centres had been under his control as head of the NKVD.
[2] A famous Soviet educator.

monastery standing on a low hill. On the way, Kartashov explained to me that their colony held first place in a nation-wide competition between colonies of its kind, that its activists' group[1] was very powerful and I should behave myself well and study and work hard.

We walked up to the gates which were opened for us. Kartashov instructed Lyudmila Sergeevna to take me to the hostel. Everybody there was already asleep. There were five or six people to a room. I was shown to a bed, where I lay down and fell peacefully asleep on a clean sheet, for the first time in a year and a half.

When I awoke in the morning, the hostel was empty. I went out into the corridor, where Lyudmila Sergeevna spotted me and told me to go and take a shower. I had a good shower, then she took me to the dining-hall, near the largest of the monastery buildings. On the way she told me something about the colony.

It had been in existence for over five years. Not all the juveniles sent there for correction had actually been convicted by a court. The ones who had not been convicted were for the most part under the age of twelve. The colony was considered disciplinary because among its members there were recidivists and escape risks. As was the case in other colonies, some of the prisoners in our colony belonged to the activist group, which helped keep order. It was made up of second-grade thieves, who did not observe the laws of the rogues' subculture, nor enjoy its privileges. As there were significantly more of them than there were 'thoroughbred' thieves, the second-grade thieves, who had the administration on their side, almost invariably came out on top at the end of the day. From time to time, however, real battles would flare up between these two groups.

In January 1938, two large batches of prisoners from Moscow and Leningrad came to the colony one after the other. These batches contained many so-called 'honest thieves'.[2] A couple of

---

[1] i.e. activist in helping the administration, putting over the official line etc.
[2] In this work the English word thief translates the Russian 'vor' and rogue translates the Russian 'zhulik'. In the Russian and Soviet

days after their arrival, the chairman of the activists' group, a 'bitchified'[1] thief, nicknamed Chervonets suggested to the new arrivals that they join one of the colony committees. There were several committees in the colony: a production committee, a hygiene committee, a recreation committee. By joining a committee one became part of the activists' group, which was absolutely unacceptable to the newly-arrived rogues. That evening, by mutual agreement, the new arrivals burst into hostel No. 7, tied up about twenty activists, barricaded the doors and hoisted from the window a white sheet with a swastika painted on it in black ink.

This was how what was known as the 'Verkhoturie shindy' began. All night it proved impossible to subdue them, and in the morning, when with the help of a fireman's ladder, the storming of the building began, the insurgents tossed tied-up activists into the faces of anyone, activists, counsellors or guards, who tried to climb the ladder. There were no serious injuries among the people ejected in this way. A couple, I think, had broken bones. The new arrivals held out in the hostel for three days, bellowing slogans which made it clear that the rogues would never join the activists. They were eventually pacified with the help of firehoses, all tied up, loaded on to lorries and carted off to Sverdlovsk. Some of them came back to the colony a week later, but twenty or so of the ringleaders were put under investigation and charged under Article 58 with instigating an uprising.

While they were in the Sverdlovsk prison, two of them committed a murder as a protest against being charged under a political article.[2] Three of them who were in another cell sawed

---

underworld both 'vory' and 'zhuliki' have codes of conduct and dependent on their adherence to these codes can be either 'honest' or 'bitchified'. A 'vor' simply operates on a more imposing scale than a 'zhulik'.
[1] A thief who as a result of betraying someone had been rejected by the thieves' community and begun collaborating with the administration. The person is called 'suka' in Russian, i.e. a bitch, the process – 'suchit'sya' to become a bitch or 'bitchified' i.e. lapsed.
[2] 'Honest' thieves and rogues are traditionally apolitical. It is only their own code which matters to them.

through the throat of some gipsy with a broken food bowl. The investigation under Article 58 was stopped, and they were convicted of murder.

Back at the camp the activists crushed the residue of malcontents one at a time and subjected them to frightful beatings-up. They were forced to kiss the activists' feet, which for them meant loss of honour, and prevented them from returning to the world of 'honest rogues'. Thereafter they became confederates of the activists and on the very next day wrought retribution on their comrades of yesterday with even greater zest than the activists themselves would have shown. Thus, in the space of about a month, everybody was coerced into joining the activists.

Everybody in the colony worked for four hours a day in one of two shifts, and also studied for four hours. The colony produced hand-winnowing machines. I was put in the smelting shop, where I worked first as an apprentice moulder, and later as a moulder. The daily quota was high and I did not fulfill it. Because we were working in a hot workshop, we were allowed a daily ration of half a litre of milk. In the school I joined the eighth class, which contained three other people who had been sentenced simply for being their parents' children. There was Volodya Bauman, son of a member of the Central Committee of the CPSU,[1] Kolya Ukhov, son of an official of the Sverdlovsk Regional Party Committee, and Mischa Medved, son of the Leningrad NKVD chief. They had all been given five years.

Mischa and I became friendly. He told me that on the day[2]

---

[1] K. Ya. Bauman, formerly a Candidate Member of the Politburo, was shot on 14 October 1937.
[2] The murder of Sergei Kirov, Member of the Politburo and Secretariat, and First Secretary of the Leningrad Party Organisation, on 1 December 1934 was the starting point and original pretext for the whole of the great purge. A series of oppositionists were shot for procuring the crime. But it now appears certain that Stalin was, in fact, responsible: the assassin, Nikolayev, whose motive was simply to strike a blow against the Party bureaucracy, was secretly aided and given his opportunity by Leonid Zaporozhets, Assistant Head of the Leningrad NKVD, on instructions from Moscow. The full story has never officially been told in Russia.

of Kírov's murder, all power in Leningrad had been transferred to the military. So it was, in fact, my uncle, Ilya Ivanovich Garkavy, at that time Deputy Commander of the Leningrad Military District, who was in control of the city. On the following day all officials of the NKVD were dismissed from their posts and no longer even allowed inside the 'big house'[1] where Nikolayev[2] was being interrogated in Stalin's presence. As I learnt later, even Yagoda, chief of the USSR NKVD, was ejected from the interrogation room. When he came into the office Stalin asked: 'What's he doing here?' Yagoda was nonplussed, left the room, returned to Moscow and, thinking that he would be arrested, stayed away from work for ten days. No one, however, was appointed in his place and he went on working for a short time.

After my own release, I met Medved's second deputy, a man called Fomin, who for some inexplicable reason survived, and in the '60s published a book called *A Chekist's Notes*, about his work during the Civil War. He is a cunning fellow, who apparently knows a great deal. He did not, however, give any interesting information at the hearings of the commission to investigate the 'Kirov affair', conducted by the Central Committee Party Control Commission. However he did give me the following details in private conversation.

Kirov was killed on 1 December 1934, at about four o'clock in the afternoon, next to his own office and Chudov's[3] office, when he was on the point of entering Chudov's office. The first person to arrive on the scene was Fomin. Nikolayev lay unconscious beside Kirov. Fomin was the first person to interrogate Nikolayev, who during the first interrogation said nothing, but simply asked to have two envelopes, confiscated during a search of his flat and each containing 500 roubles, passed on to his wife and to his mother. There was also some note from Nikolayev

---

[1] The popular name for the HQ of the Leningrad NKVD and the present-day KGB, equivalent to Moscow's Lubyanka.
[2] The murderer of Kirov.
[3] Mikhail Chudov, Second Secretary of the Leningrad Party Organisation. He was shot in 1937.

to his wife, of whose contents Fomin stubbornly refused to speak. Late that evening, Agranov, I think it was, flew into Leningrad and at once took the investigation out of Fomin's hands. Fomin also said that Nikolayev wept and vomited all the time. He had earlier drunk a great deal of beer – this fact was established by an expert medical examination. I heard too that at the first interrogation in the presence of Stalin, who had arrived in Leningrad on 2 December with Molotov and Voroshilov, Nikolayev turned to one of the persons there and shouted: 'But you promised me . . .' At that moment someone struck him on the head with the butt of a pistol.

In Moscow I talked to Batner,[1] who was a member of the Collegium which had tried Nikolayev. Batner himself handed Nikolayev the indictment before the trial. He said that Nikolayev was the only person at the trial who pleaded guilty and incriminated others. None of the rest pleaded guilty and all stated that they didn't even know Nikolayev. I asked Batner: 'Don't you think that Nikolayev was a man of straw?' He was surprised by my question and replied: 'I never thought of that, but Nikolayev's behaviour even then made me rather surprised. He behaved quite calmly in court and did a lot of talking.'

While I am about it, I will pass on all that Batner said on other matters too.

He told me that my father and his co-accused had been tried on the second floor of the building of the Military Collegium, where the city military registration and enlistment office now is. Batner was clerk of the court on that occasion. Frinovsky, Yezhov's deputy, ran the whole thing. In the hall behind the accused were two armchairs in which Yegorov, chief of the General Staff[2] and Orlov,[3] Naval Chief of Staff (arrested on the day after this trial) were sitting. The whole building and the hall itself were under a military guard armed with rifles.

[1] Military Jurist First Rank A. A. Batner. He was Secretary of the Court in various trials, including that of Bukharin.
[2] Marshal Yegorov was himself shot either on 22 February 1939, or on 10 March 1941. (Soviet sources disagree on the date.)
[3] Admiral Orlov was shot in a great massacre of political and military leaders which took place from 27 to 29 July 1938.

There were ten or so high-ranking commanders in the hall as well. He did not remember who they were. The trial went smoothly. Two or three abstract questions were put to each of the accused. Ulrikh, the Chairman of the Military Collegium of the Supreme Court, asked all the questions, consulting for form's sake with members of the Special Session. These were Budyonny, Dybenko, Shaposhnikov, Blyukher, Alksnis, Kashirin, Belov and Goryachov. (Goryachov shot himself soon after.)

There were only two hitches in the trial. One was when Blyukher, explaining that he had a stomach complaint, requested permission to leave. They took the sentence to his home for him to sign. The second occurred after Shaposhnikov's question to Uborevich: 'Yeronim Petrovich, would you say that the bad defence of the Pinsk Marshes was a trap you set for the Germans intentionally? You wanted to lure them on and then surround them?' Ulrikh tut-tutted at Shaposhnikov and ordered Uborevich not to answer. According to what Batner said, my father was asked: 'Did you know that the officer appointed to look after you during your training in Germany was a German Intelligence officer?' My father answered that he had no doubt of this at all, but he elicited information from the officer and not vice versa.

Before the end of the court hearing my father demanded that Stalin should be invited to attend the trial, since he thought that Stalin knew nothing of what was going on. Primakov[1] was quick to reply that not only did Stalin know about the whole thing, but it was he in fact who had arranged it all.

The trial lasted about four hours. After the sentence was pronounced, the prisoners joined hands and sang the *Internationale*. The commandant of the Special Session was Yegorov. All the stories about how people behaved when the sentence was carried out came from his adjutant. Batner was a member of the Military Collegium the whole time. He was present in that same building in the autumn of 1941 during the trial of Pavlov[2]

[1] Corps Commander Primakov had been under arrest since the autumn of 1936.
[2] Army General D. G. Pavlov commanded the Western Front in the

and others. According to his account, all the papers and sentences with Stalin's and others' instructions written on them, Ulrikh kept in a safe. He never let anyone see these documents, nor did the members of the Military Collegium ask him anything about them.

Immediately after Kirov's murder, the law was published concerning the conduct of cases of persons charged with terrorism, which had already been signed by Kalinin on 1 December 1934. How did it come about that on the day of Kirov's murder, when the investigation of the case was still not complete, this unconstitutional law had already been signed? This is what it said:

1. The investigation of cases of terrorism must be completed within ten days.
2. The court sits in camera, without the participation of counsel.
3. The death sentence is mandatory, not subject to appeal and is carried out immediately after the trial.[1]

Subsequently many thousands of people were executed under this law. From Stalin's point of view it was very convenient, since it permitted him to dispatch honest men to the next world quickly and without fuss. I think that this law had been prepared earlier, but that a pretext was needed for it to be introduced. This indirectly confirms that Kirov was killed on Stalin's orders. The guard who allegedly was too far behind Kirov was killed at once, on his way to the first interrogation.[2] Afterwards the escort who had killed him were also shot. This

---

initial stages of the German invasion in 1941. He was thereupon shot, with most of his leading subordinates, on charges of treason.

[1] Yakir has here conflated the 1 December 1934 decree proper with defining regulations put out at about the same time.

[2] Kirov's guard, Borisov, was being brought to interrogation in the back of a truck. The NKVD man in the front seized the steering wheel, so that the truck hit a wall at low speed. It was announced that Borisov had been killed in this 'accident': but he was in fact beaten to death with iron bars by the two NKVD men in the back with him.

was mentioned at the 20th Party Congress, but no one there remarked on the fact that the guard came to Leningrad from Moscow with Zaporozhets,[1] who had been recommended by Stalin to Kirov for the job of Leningrad NKVD chief. When Kirov did not agree to this appointment Zaporozhets was nevertheless made Medved's First Deputy. When, after the murder, a list was compiled of NKVD employees who were to be prosecuted for negligence, Zaporozhets' name was not included in the first version, but was inserted only after its absence had been noticed by Voroshilov. Each of these NKVD officials got three years. Medved worked as chief of an administration in the Kolyma.[2] In 1937 however they were all shot, with the exception of Fomin. After the law of December 1st had been passed, during a single month there was conducted a series of trials of 'terrorists' who had suddenly sprung up in Leningrad, Moscow, Kiev and Minsk. In all 119 people were shot.

But we must get back to Verkhoturie.

Amateur entertainment was a feature of life in the colony. Everybody had to take part in some group or other. Initially I joined the accordionists' group, but after learning several tunes by heart with a deal of difficulty, I transferred to the drama group, which was preparing to stage a play called *The Pioneer's Post*. I knew that the play would be put on outside the compound for the civilian population. Getting out of the compound was something I dreamed of doing, and I decided to escape.

One day in May 1939, the amateur entertainers left the compound to give a concert in the local orphanage. In the play I took the part of a colonel, the officer in charge of the post. It took several days to persuade the people in charge of the colony to agree to my leaving the compound. I was, however, the only person who had been learning the colonel's part and conse-

---

[1] Leonid Zaporozhets, the NKVD officer responsible for seeing that the assassin had access to Kirov, seems to have been shot in 1937 or 1938.
[2] The Kolyma camp complex in North-Eastern Siberia was one of the most feared and most deadly. Some two million people are believed to have died there.

quently Lyudmila Sergeevna and Marusya, a girl from outside, who was leader of our Pioneer group, insisted on my being allowed out. The authorities eventually agreed, but demanded that Lyudmila Sergeevna and Marusya gave a written acceptance of responsibility. Marusya and I were good friends. When we had left the compound, Marusya said: 'Of course I know you might get up to something. Do whatever you like. I love you and have no regrets at having stood guarantor for you.'

After the first act, during the interval, when everybody had gone up on to the first floor, I leaped out of the window of the make-up room on the ground floor and made off towards the river for all I was worth. I spotted a rowing boat on the bank, got into it and crossed to the far bank. From Marusya's stories, I knew that on the far bank there was a deserted windmill. I had to fight my way through scrub for about three hours before emerging into a large clearing where I saw the windmill.

I had run away in my shirtsleeves and spent the whole night shivering with cold, unable to get even a moment's sleep. Dawn came and I wondered whether to wait for Marusya (I had managed to let Mischa Medved know that I would wait for her at the windmill) or whether to press on. Although I did not know the neighbourhood, I did know for sure that there were many camps in the area. This meant I might walk straight from one camp into another. I began to try and work out in which direction the railway line lay. While I was absorbed in these thoughts morning came. Suddenly Marusya appeared from a coppice. I ran to meet her and deluged her with questions. She told me sadly, that as soon as it became known that I had run away, all the amateur entertainers were herded back into the colony, and all the guards sent off to hunt for me. In a fury Kartashov telephoned the warden of the camp section of Sevurallag[1] in Verkhutorie, and camp guards also set off looking for me. Marusya brought me food and warm clothing and explained to me how to reach the Irbit highway, where I could get a lift on a lorry as far as the Irbit railway. She recommended

[1] Upravleniye Severno–Uralskikh Lagerei, the administration of camps in the northern Urals.

me not to go through any inhabited areas, since in those districts where there were camps the local people willingly handed fugitives over to the authorities because they got a reward for doing so. She said they were looking for me in the area of the railway. We kissed and parted.

I went through the forest. It was very damp underfoot, but what saved me was the fact that I had a pair of good non-prison boots on my feet. I hardly stopped at all for about eight hours. My legs ached with fatigue. On only one occasion did I have to make a detour through the forest to avoid some village. There was still no sign whatever of the highway. After slaking my thirst with brackish water and taking a short rest, I moved on. Towards evening I came out into some sort of cutting with a road running through it. As I later discovered this was in fact the Irbit highway. There was no traffic on the highway and the road was bad. After some time I heard the noise of an engine. A vehicle was approaching me from behind. I retreated at once into the forest: knowing the morals of the local population I was afraid to flag the driver down. The lorry drove past and once again all was silent. My situation seemed hopeless and I had already begun to despair. It was my second day without sleep, I was tired out and Irbit was about 200 kilometres away. After walking for about another hour, I saw ahead of me the faintly glimmering lights of a village, and to one side several hay ricks. I was overjoyed, went over to one of the ricks, lifted up the side of it; climbed in and covered myself with hay. I fell fast asleep.

When I woke up it was daytime already and the sun was shining brightly. I climbed out of the rick and began to shake the hay off myself. I turned towards the road and saw three men approaching. One of them had a dog on a lead. The dog was panting and straining to get at me, but the handler kept it up. (I later heard of dogs being set on fugitives and savaging their prey during a chase like this.) I recognised a senior counsellor from our colony, Dmitri Ivanovich. The dog handler stopped and the other two came up to me. The other chap, a camp guard, wanted to strike me, but Dmitri Ivanovich would not allow him to. 'These punks who skedaddle and you have to go poking about in the swamps for them day and night,' muttered the camp guard. 'If he were one of ours, we wouldn't bring him back alive.'

'Well, you've covered some ground,' said Dmitri Ivanovich. 'Come on then.'

Three kilometres from that spot a lorry was waiting for us. They put me in the back and sat waiting for someone. The camp guard fired three times into the air and about an hour and a half later two more groups, also accompanied by dogs, came back from the hunt to the lorry. They climbed aboard, dogs and all, and the engine burst into life. It was already getting dark when we got back to the colony.

Kartashov and Lyudmila Sergeevna were standing on the porch. When I walked up to him he asked me in a surly manner: 'Well then? You got tired of living? Can you hear what's going on in the compound? (From the compound I could hear a rumble of voices and a huge crowd of kids had gathered by the guardhouse to await my arrival.) Do you realise that because of your escape our colony's dropped from first place down to twenty-ninth in the competition? (An escape was regarded as the most heinous 'infringement' of all.) If I let you go into the compound now, the lads will tear you apart. Well what do you say? Are you going?'

I agreed without thinking. I entered the compound. There were about 200 people standing near the guardhouse, with our block elder, Chervonets, lurking in the middle of them. The crowd was very angry. People kept shouting 'bitch', 'bastard'. No one made a move however. Mischa Medved came over to me. He openly took from his sleeve a large knife made from a file, handed it to me and took his place beside me. Turning to Chervonets I said in a calm voice: 'I've nothing in common with any of you, thieves or activists. If you want to beat me up because we've dropped down to 29th place then go ahead and beat me to death. But unless you finish me off, Chervonets, I shall cut your throat.'

He muttered something in reply.

Bauman and Ukhov stood near by clutching something in their sleeves. I looked round and noticed that behind my boys some twenty or so other likely lads were standing. As I learned later, they had arrived from the Moscow children's prison Danilovka the day before my escape. Our activists hadn't had time to work them over and it was clear that if anything were to have started then, they would have come in on my side.

The activists realised this too. The crowd threw out a few more filthy expletives and began to disperse.

Kartashov stood by the guardhouse and watched the whole thing. When everybody had gone, he told me to come into the guardhouse building.

'You're going to the camp prison now, and tomorrow we'll have a talk,' he said in a menacing tone.

The camp prison was two kilometres away from the compound. I was escorted there by guards. The building was empty. I was there on my own. The next day I was sent for. In the duty room I was met by Kartashov, and a man in civilian clothes whom I did not know. Kartashov put the questions and the stranger took notes.

'Why did you do this?'

'Because I've been imprisoned for nothing. Children do not answer for their parents. I myself have committed no crime and consequently want to be free.'

'You could always make a complaint if you feel you've been wrongly convicted. It's the second time you've tried to escape you know. We could try you for it.'

'There's a maximum of three years under Article 82,[1] so in principle, if the sentences are to run concurrently, I've got more than three years to go as it is.'

'Yes, but if you were to be tried under Article 82, you'd be in "disciplinary" colonies; you'd never see it through.'

'Do you know the words of the song they composed on the Solovki Islands: "Better once to take the risk than be in tor-

[1] Article 82 of the Soviet Criminal Code provides for up to three years' imprisonment as punishment for an escape.

ment for three years. Either death or freedom, that's all the choice you have."'

Kartashov looked at me sadly and said: 'Well, it's your own affair . . . But what didn't suit you here?'

After that the man in mufti suddenly started asking the questions: 'Where were you escaping to? And who are your contacts outside?'

'I didn't know where I was escaping to. I was escaping from prison and I haven't got any contacts outside. All my relations are in prison. I don't even know where they are. There's just my old grandfather in Odessa who sends me parcels.'

'Have you sent any letters out of here via illegal channels?'

'Good God. There's no need to start an investigation like the one in '37. Perhaps you're going to ask me whether I was in contact with the Japanese Intelligence Service?'

The man in mufti became angry and I was taken back to the cell, where I remained for four days. The guards in the camp prison were relatively polite and the food was good, but there was nothing to do there. I thought a great deal about myself and about my escapes. Three days passed in this way. On the third day Marusya unexpectedly came into the cell. I was very glad to see her. We chatted for a while and then said goodbye.

Another person I saw in the prison was Lyudmila Sergeevna. She told me that Kartashov had sent a report to Sverdlovsk and to Moscow about the whole thing, and had got permission to send me to a maximum security camp. I asked her all sorts of questions about her life, which she willingly answered. We parted as friends.

On the fifth day I heard sounds of some kind of activity outside the door and Mischa Medved came into the cell. He told me that he had been sent for at work and escorted to the prison. Before that he had been to the store and to the hostel where I lived, and both his things and mine had been brought to the prison on a cart. This confirmed what Lyudmila Sergeevna had said, that we were really being sent off somewhere. Mischa talked of the mood in the compound. The likely lads who had come from Moscow were setting the tone, criticising the activists for collaborating with the camp security officers; friars[1] like me made escapes, while they, who had once had real rogue's blood in their veins, actually narked for the authorities.

He also told me that Volodya Bauman and Kolya Ukhov had been left in the colony and were now quite on their own.

The next morning some guards came from our colony, and we were sent for. The guards loaded all our things on to a cart, and took us to the station. When we got there the escort commander bought the tickets. The train arrived and again, without any help from us, our things were loaded on to it. We were taken into the carriage. A separate compartment in an ordinary carriage had been set aside for us and our escort. We made ourselves comfortable and the train moved off.

Passengers kept looking into our compartment with a certain amount of surprise: two kids under escort was not a common sight. All around, as is usually the case in railway carriages, people were getting out their parcels and in fact one person had already started eating. We too were very hungry. We put this to the escort commander. He said that our journey would only last for two and a half hours, but if we had any money, then we could buy something to eat at a station. We had in fact been given all that we had in our account. After we left the next station some food appeared on the little table in our compartment; bread, butter, sausage and even some vodka. The guards ate with us. We quickly got tipsy and lay down to sleep. The guards chatted with the passengers. It seemed to me that I had no sooner laid down than we had arrived at our destination. We got down from the carriage. On the station building was written 'Iss Station'.

We had to travel seven kilometres to our destination. The guards carried all our things. Eventually we saw the four-storey building of a prison and next to it on one side a huge compound, approximately two kilometres wide, a very high fence about ten metres high and in front of the fence a twelve-metre wide restricted area which had been ploughed up and raked over.

[1] A friar – a pejorative term for someone who does not belong to the underworld fraternity – possibly from Yiddish, or even English.

Along the top of the fence, stretched on special brackets projecting from both sides, was barbed wire. In the middle of the fence were gates and a small guardhouse. This was the Nizhnyaya Tura maximum security colony and beside it was the Nizhnyaya Tura prison.

4
Nizhnyaya Tura

The escort commander went into the guardhouse and we sat down near by on our belongings. About an hour later he returned with two men in uniform. One of them was the colony duty warder and the other, a tall man with the face of an intellectual, the governor of the colony, whose name was Otto. The governor said to Mischa and me: 'All your things are to go into store. If anyone tries to take advantage of you, you can reach me via any of the warders.'

'All right, Citizen Governor,' we answered. When he was about to leave, he asked, addressing me directly, 'Do you remember your father?'

'I remember him very well.'

Then the duty warder checked our personal data under the twenty headings on our camp passport, after which we picked up our 'clobber' and went into the compound. Straight in front of us was a huge hut which was the dining-hall. On the left, in a corner, separated from the compound by a high fence topped with barbed wire, was the punishment block. On the right, also fenced off, was another large hut, the BUR.[1] Immediately behind the BUR was the store, where we handed in our things and an inventory of them was made. Then we were taken to the bath-house. We went into the changing room, hung our clothing on wire rings to be roasted and got ready to go and bathe. The bath-house attendant opened the door into the bath-house and began chasing out the people who were using it: 'That's enough, that'll do. You've got all the dirt off,' he shouted. In response to these remarks came the squealing

---

[1] Barak usilennovo rezhima, intensified discipline hut. After the punishment cell the next sanction in the scale of punishments: a prisoner can be put there for longer periods, of up to three months.

voices of a lot of women. I glanced with curiosity into the bath-house and saw a large number of naked females. The bath attendant chased them out to get dressed, and Mischa and I went into the bath-house. It was a huge bath-house, with about 100 taps and a good steam room. We started to get washed and then climbed into the steam bath. Some time later the bath attendant discovered us and chased us off to get dressed. He rang for the duty warder, who then took us to the dining-hall.

We had something to eat and went to our hut. The hut was divided into three dormitories. There was an entrance at each end and a third one in the middle at which we entered. Over the door were the figures 7/2, i.e. dormitory No. 2 of hut No. 7. We went inside and saw that all the walls were taken up with single-tier plank beds, on which kids of roughly our own age were lying. The fact that the warder had appeared made no impression on them whatsoever. The warder shouted loudly: 'Goldie!' A youth a little older than we were popped out from somewhere round a corner. He was dressed in long cotton underpants, box-calf boots, a shirt with a side fastening at the neck and a waistcoat. 'What's that, citizen boss?'

'I've brought you two new lads from Verkhoturie. See you don't do them any harm.' Goldie wagged his head in reply and the duty warder left. All the denizens of the dormitory at once crowded round us. Among them were some lads who had come from Verkhoturie not long before us. One of them, Lyosha, the gipsy, shook hands with us and said to Goldie: 'These are the chaps I was telling you about.' Goldie turned to us in a friendly manner and pointed to a place near him on the plank bunks. We made ourselves comfortable. The others stayed around and we had to tell them about Verkhoturie and about my escape. When we were talking about the Verkhoturie activists, many of them expressed indignation and said that one fine day they would cut all those bitches' throats.

While we were telling our tale, a very well-dressed fellow of thirty-five or so entered the hut, and coming over to Goldie, said: 'Well, what are you lot up to? Perhaps we can have a bit of fun.' Goldie smartly pulled out from underneath his pillow a pack of home-made cards, squatted down Turkish style, put a small cushion in front of him and in a playful tone observed: 'Well, sit down then, Wizard, and I'll make you disappear.'

Wizard elegantly hitched up his pants, kicked off his shoes and sat down opposite in the same pose as Goldie: 'All the way – hard for hard.' (All the way meant they would play Stoss, and hard for hard that they would [both] be playing for hard cash). The game began, with everybody watching. Half an hour later Wizard had lost fifty roubles in money to Goldie and then offered his jacket as a stake.

'Keep your togs for your own back,' Goldie answered. Wizard got up and his parting shot was: 'Don't worry, I'll have you in your birthday suit before I'm through. I'll skin you right down to your pigeons.'[1]

'Go and get your pinching done before the trams stop,' Goldie replied (which in underworld jargon means 'On your way').

Goldie handed the money he had won to the Gipsy and said: 'Well, my dear chap, perhaps you can think of something.' The Gipsy disappeared forthwith and an hour later turned up with ten little bottles of concentrated eau de cologne. Goldie rubbed his hands and invited us to participate in the feast. Sausage, pork fat and honey cake appeared. We had a drink. It was the first time I had drunk eau de cologne and water. It had a pale, milky colour, and when you belched afterwards – it was like being freshened up at the hairdressers. A glass of eau de cologne made your head spin.

At this point a stocky kid with a guitar came into the hut. Goldie called him over, addressing him as Zaika Shumsky, and offered him a glass of eau de cologne. Shumsky drank it down, took some food and sang a song which I'd never heard before. The song was about a game of Stoss. I fell asleep to its melody and awoke when we were roused for the count. In Nizhnyaya Tura the count was done in the same way as subsequently in the special camps after 1948, i.e. the prisoners were first lined up and counted and then had to come forward when their

[1] Underwear.

names were called. After the count, Mischa and I declined a drink of tea, lay down and were soon snoring once again.

In the Nizhnyaya Tura colony there were twelve large huts with three dormitories in each. In the middle sections like ours there were fifty persons and one hundred each in the side ones. In all there were about 3,000 people in the compound. There were two women's huts. There was also the working area, which at that time was not fenced off from the living area. There were two kinds of work in the working area, a timber plant embracing all the processes involved in producing barrel staves, boards for packing cases, and planing large planks square, and also a factory which made beds for the army and for the camps. The factory had a forge, an assembly shop and a mechanical repair shop. There was no work which involved leaving the compound. Anybody who wanted to could work. The rest, to which number I belonged, did not go to work, by reason of what was described as their 'lack of footwear and clothing'. The fact of the matter was that we declined the offer of prison uniform available from the store, hid our own trousers and went about in our underwear. The authorities did not make us wear prison uniform and go to work. All this was because most of the people in Nizhnyaya Tura were recidivists, with either three or more convictions or a conviction for escaping.

There were in fact people who had been in prison on political charges since 1918 or 1919. One of them was Admiral Kolchak's[1] former finance minister, who always had his term extended – never for more than five years, but he was not released. He worked as an orderly in the shoe repairing shop and was an unsociable man with strange ways. He would for example collect his midday meal in a pan, bring it to his room (he lived separately), put on an apron, place a towel over his arm, pour the food into a plate and place it on the table with a dignified bow. He would then remove the towel from his arm, take off the apron and sit down at the table. When he had finished his lunch he once again transformed himself into a servant and

[1] For a time commander-in-chief of the White forces in the Civil War.

cleared the table. The rogues thought that since he'd been a finance minister he must have amassed a lot of money and in his absence they combed his whole room, but they found nothing.

Sergei Stepanchenko was also in this camp. He had, I think, formerly been the governor of the town of Pskov and had fought with the forces of Yudenich.[1] He had escaped several times and was later arrested for taking part in the Antonov uprising in 1921.[2] He had been given a five-year term and put in one of the first camps in the USSR, at Krasnaya Vishera, not far from Solikamsk. (This is now called Noryplag and is the place where Anatoli Marchenko[3] is serving his sentence.) He escaped from there, was caught and sent to the Solovki Islands where the famous hangman of Solovki, a man called Kurilko, was in command. Stepanchenko used to say that when a batch of prisoners arrived, Kurilko himself checked the new arrivals. He stood them in a single line and shouted in a loud voice: 'Thieves, one step forward! Prostitutes, two steps forward! Speculators, three! Priests, four! Counter-revolutionaries, five! Anybody here in Solovki for the second time, step to the side!' The last category he would house in normal conditions, but forced all the rest to work eighteen hours a day in the cold on a poor diet. This was more than most people could stand and many died . . .

There were cases of the guards committing murder and subjecting the prisoners to ridicule. This gave rise to the following song:

> *Oh, Moscow, where have you led us?*
> *How great the grief you have brought us:*
> *Laid bare our guilt for all to see*
> *Rewarded us with Solovki,*
> *Oh why did our mother bear us?*

[1] Leading White general in the Civil War.
[2] The Antonov rebellion, centred on Tambov in the Volga Basin, was a large-scale peasant uprising led by Social Revolutionaries.
[3] On 29 July 1971, after this book was written, Anatoli Marchenko was released from prison, having served his sentence. He has since been rearrested.

Far off Sekir Gora hangs its head
O'er the hosts of distant nameless dead
Where the wild wind blows,
No mother knows
Where her son has laid his head.

The darkling forest saw every one
Of the many miracles that there were done
On the stumps they stood us,
Stripped us and flogged us,
And then the boss called us 'dung'.

Stepanchenko however survived. He was a tough, strong courageous man. At the beginning of the 1930s he was sent from Solovki to Gorshorlag, near Kemerovo, where a high road was being built. He told us that there the law of 'reforging' was still enforced, i.e. they had a shot at re-educating people. Jokers, for example, from the camp administration, when it was pouring with rain, drove the lags out to work, forcing them to carry slogans which said 'It is not raining on the highway!' Stepanchenko escaped from there too. Once again he was caught – a nation-wide search was instituted. After spending several years in prison, Stepanchenko ended up at Nizhnyaya Tura. Here too he endeavoured to escape. He made himself a folding iron ladder in the works and flinging it on to the fence, charged up it, but was wounded in the leg and fell into the restricted area. After that, he spent a year in solitary in a top-security prison for political prisoners. One floor of this prison was set aside for lags who had infringed colony discipline. To be put in there was the most severe punishment of all.

In Nizhnyaya Tura, just like everywhere else, there was a punishment block where people were put for from thirty to forty-five days; the BUR, where they were held up to three months; and then it was the 'block', i.e. the top-security political prison. Lags were punished for insulting the administration, for playing cards, for murders, for causing bodily harm and for being caught with women. One wasn't put in the punishment block for 'industrial' offences.¹ When I got to know Stepanchenko, he had already recovered from his period in solitary and moustaches twitching, was once again thinking about escaping. 'As long as I live,' he said, 'I shall try to escape.'

There were about 1,000 'honest' rogues at Nizhnyaya Tura. This was a large number even for a camp. The whole camp played cards. The rogues' laws, which by this time had begun to break down in other camps, still held good. In a word the rogues here lived as they wanted to live.

Apart from the rogues' fraternity, there was at Nizhnyaya Tura a sizeable group of physically abnormal and mentally sick persons. There were for example about ten 'hermaphrodites'. One of them went about in men's clothing and was called Marya Ivanovna, another wore women's clothes and was known as Uncle Katya. Their lives were unhappy. Neither the men nor the women accepted them and they didn't even get on well with one another.

In Nizhnyaya Tura there were about fifty gipsy men and women – inveterate thieves and scoundrels. Because however, there were plenty of real rogues even without them, they were regarded as a second-rate rogues' fraternity, and were obliged to cheat each other. The rest of the company was made up of escapees and camp murderers, many of whom were doing their first stretch.

During my whole time there only one fresh batch of prisoners came to the camp. At the beginning of 1938, about two hundred men and women sentenced under article 58, arrived from Moscow. Nobody could understand why they had been sent there. They were ordinary people who had been wrongfully convicted. Among them was a beautiful nineteen-year-old Polish girl called Wanda Benakh. She had been given ten years simply because her parents lived in Poland. She and I became friends. Wanda did an unskilled job at the timber processing plant. The manager, a man called Dugin, who was not a prisoner, pursued her for a long time, but she made no response to his

¹ i.e. failing to fulfil the quota, minor damage to machinery, waste of materials.

efforts at courting and his promises to help her to live well in the camp. Dugin began to take revenge on her. He swindled her cruelly over her work rates, and her rations were reduced accordingly. She accepted all this, but Dugin was relentless and he transferred her to the latrine squad. I once said to her: 'To hell with all this, he'll starve you to death.' She made no reply.

As a punishment for playing cards I landed in the punishment block, where I spent thirty days on 300 grammes of bread daily, and skilly once in three days. Thirty days later I staggered, totally exhausted, back to our hut. First they gave me a good meal and then told me that the Moscow girl thief, Lyalka the Ballerina, had dropped in several times. I asked Mischa to go to the women's hut and find out what she wanted. When he got back Mischa said that Wanda wanted to see me. I set off for the women's hut. Wanda came out to speak to me and asked me to come to her that night. She had decided to let Dugin have his way, but did not want him to have her while she was still a virgin. I told her that I had only that same day emerged from the punishment block and was right on my last legs, but she didn't want to listen. The idea was deeply fixed in her mind that her first man ought not to be a camp boss. I liked Wanda a great deal, but found such prosaicness very embarrassing. Nevertheless I went to her after lights out.

On the next day I again landed in the punishment block. In camp the punishment block is called the 'izo', 'shizo',[1] 'hold' or 'kandey'.[2] About five days later at night the door of the cell opened and the duty warder woke me up and gave me a large bag. In it were two loaves of bread, some tobacco and about a kilo of sugar. I realised that Wanda had kept to her decision and had made Dugin agree to help me.

In the punishment block the rogues stopped at nothing. They took the bread ration from muzhiks[3] and friars, made fools of

---

[1] Abbreviations for 'shtrafoni izolyator', literally penal isolator.
[2] Kandey – probably a corrupted form of 'kandaly' manacles.
[3] Muzhik – the Russian word for a peasant, here used in an underworld jargon sense as a person not initiated in the ways of the underworld, but who in contrast to a 'friar' might make it given time.

them on the principle, 'Let everyone else kick the bucket so long as we don't.' One friar was put into the punishment block for stealing something from the kitchen. The rogues began to question him about what he did before he was arrested. It transpired that he had been a policeman. Their delight knew no bounds: 'A real live policeman, here in the cell!' They made him walk on all fours and mumble, 'A goat walking on the road found a three-legged billy goat'; then he had to repeat several times, 'I shall butt you', whereupon they hit him on the head with a boot and answered, 'I'm not afraid.'

I would also like to tell the story of how I cleaned out[1] Nizhnyaya Tura. Although I was a young friar, i.e. I did not enjoy the privileges of the rogues' fraternity, in so far as I hobnobbed with Goldie and the Gipsy, the camp rogues treated me with respect. Juveniles were issued with a kilogram of sugar a month. In the cards market this ration was worth one rouble. On one occasion, just before we got our sugar ration, an adult thief called Vasya the Beast nipped into our hut and suggested we play a hand of cards for my sugar. Adults only got a third of the amount we did. (His own stake was in money.) Right from the start I had good hands and won from him twenty-five roubles cash, a good suit, a pair of boots, a feather pillow and also some underwear. I didn't bother to claim the underwear, and was on the point of going to the stores to fetch my sugar when some rogue from the Beast's gang skipped into the hut, and the game started up again. I played on without sleep for almost three days and nights in a row, against a succession of partners who turned up. I already had at my disposal a vast sum of money and put such a high stake on the first card that I was able to beat any contestant. An enormous number of fans followed the course of the game. Ultimately the rogues of Nizhnyaya Tura lost to me everything they possessed. I had amassed more than 16,000 roubles, about 100 suits, the same number of pairs of boots and pillows and a pile of various other odds and ends. Everything was heaped in a corner and Goldie, Gipsy and

---

[1] Cleaned out – i.e. at cards.

Mischa Medved, i.e. our little commune, reclined on this pile of gear. For about two weeks we spent money like water. Every day our card-playing partners would come back bringing money or clothes they had got hold of, which we proceeded to win from them.

But my turn came too. I can't remember who suggested the game, but I do remember that the original stake was a dark silk scarf, valued at three roubles. And this, as they say, was the scarf that throttled me. They cleaned me out completely. Well, easy come, easy go.

I'll tell you now about my third attempt to escape. We decided to dig a tunnel from under our hut. There were six people actually in the group, but everyone knew about it. We spent about twenty days digging our hole, dragging the earth out of it and spreading it out underneath the floorboards. One day, when our hole already went roughly to the far side of the restricted area, Mischa Medved, Seryozha the Gipsy and I were under the floorboards digging. It was about midday. Just at that moment a general count of the whole colony was announced, at which all the prisoners, workers and non-workers, had to be present. Everybody was lined up, counted and the roll was called out and checked against the card index. We were missing from the count and someone from our hut squealed about where we were and what we were doing. Without even waiting for the end of the count, the warders dashed off to our hut and began breaking up the floor. We of course heard, but instead of coming out from under the floor, we crawled off beneath the hut in various directions and lay still, not daring to breathe. Suddenly, right above my head, someone pulled up a floorboard. I made a point of not opening my eyes. I was dragged out and kicked, but I did not react to this treatment in any way. They then decided that I had fainted and put ammonia-soaked cotton wool under my nose. This made me sneeze. I opened my eyes and was obliged to give an explanation: 'Yes, we dug that tunnel. I and the others have been imprisoned for nothing, and as long as we have the strength, we shall try to escape.'

The governor of the colony, Otto, who was present, accepted this explanation; but I was still dispatched to the punishment block. I heard soon afterwards that not only had Mischa, Gipsy and Goldie been put in the punishment block, but some other lads as well. There were only seven cells in the punishment block and the people in there before we came were granted an amnesty. That day, we weren't even informed how long we would have to stay in the punishment block, and we decided that we were under investigation. Next day, however, we got our rations – 300 grammes of bread – and to our great surprise a large piece of dry-salted hump-backed salmon.[1] We ate all this at one go and immediately got the point: the hump-backed salmon was very salty and for the next two days we weren't given any water. Our mouths dried out, our tongues became swollen and we were generally in poor physical shape. We emerged from the punishment block forty-five days later.

I went to work as an apprentice turner in the mechanical repair shop. Attached to this workshop was a provision store, whose stock for the most part consisted of sweet stuffs, cigarettes and makhorka. We decided to give the store a going-over. We got hold of the keys and one night removed a sack of gingerbreads, 200 packets of 'Zvyozdochka' cigarettes, about 100 packets of makhorka, a small amount of sugar and two 3-litre tins of condensed milk. Mischa, I and a small-time thief called Hunchback, took part in this robbery. We brought our haul back to the hut and feasted till morning. The tobacco of course we hid.

In the morning the investigation began. Hunchback gave evidence against Mischa and me and we were all three put in the investigation cell of the camp prison. The camp security officer, Petrov, summoned us for interrogation. At one of the interrogation sessions he said to me: 'I served under your father, who was a fine man, not at all like the friends you've found for yourself. They're the ones who have shopped you.'

---

[1] A fish found in the rivers of the Soviet Far East, such as the Amur and the Ussuri. Before spawning the males grow a hump on their back – hence the name.

After this session I spent a further twenty days in the camp prison. Then Mischa and I were sent for transfer. I learned later that Hunchback got five years for robbing the store. The camp security officer preferred charges against him alone as a reward for his treachery, and we were just transferred.

Once again it was a Stolypin carriage, full of teenagers and rogues from Nizhnyaya Tura, about eighty in all. Someone demanded water and got into an argument with a guard. The escort commander came and said: 'We'll get rid of that thirst for you!' They dragged out the malcontent and took him away in the direction of the lavatory. We heard a cry and about twenty minutes later he was brought back to the compartment. With great pleasure he showed us his hands, and one could see on his wrists the marks left by sharp metal teeth. Some of the marks were bleeding slightly. 'It's a new kind of American handcuff – chromium plated,' he gasped. 'Every time you try to move they sink their teeth in deeper and deeper.' We of course envied him his new experience.[1] One after another we summoned the guard to our compartment and insulted him. We were hauled out, clapped in the handcuffs for a time and brought back to the compartment. Thus in the space of a single night all the inhabitants of the compartment voluntarily underwent this punishment. The handcuffs fully lived up to our expectations.

The next day we reached the new camp, where there wasn't a single hut apart from the punishment block, but there were about 200 army tents. It was early autumn and cold. Our particulars were checked in the usual way, we were admitted to the compound, and assigned to two of the tents. We had arrived at a station called Bogoslovsk, Section 14 of Sevurallag.

[1] This bizarre reaction to something new is not uncommon among young prisoners.

5
Sevurallag

For the first fourteen days we were in quarantine. We weren't allowed to go to work and for want of anything better to do we wandered round the compound. During this period, several batches of prisoners arrived from Leningrad, Moscow and Rostov. For the most part they were rogues. They felt they ruled the roost there, as they did everywhere else in the camps, and this time they didn't give me the go-by either. A Moscow rogue called Vasyok who had arrived with us from Nizhnyaya Tura, ordered me to give him all my gear. I knew that resistance was pointless and fraught with danger, so I gave him all my things. A little while later one of the middle-aged thieves, Sasha the Yid, won all my things back from Vasyok and with him looking on returned them to me, saying impressively as he did so: 'There you are, wear 'em!' This meant that the clothes were his property and mine simply to wear, which meant that no one could take them away from me.

The first snow fell and the quarantine period ended. They started driving us out to work. Most people didn't want to leave the compound. We bunched together near the guardhouse and tried to avoid leaving the compound. Some little time later the escort guards came in through the open gates. There were about forty of them and they were unarmed. They hurled us to the ground one at a time, grabbed us by the legs and dragged us through the snow out of the compound. Outside there were escort guards armed with rifles, handlers and dogs, so one really had no alternative but to get up and go to work. They took us to a coal seam, where excavators were used for opencast mining. Even there the only thing we bothered to do was to light a campfire. The authorities had managed to get us to our place of work but they couldn't make us work.

Seeing the ineffectiveness of the escort, we went to work the next day of our own free will, having decided to escape at the first opportunity. We spent the first five days picking a convenient time and then at the end of the working day when it was already dark, five of us made off. We spent the whole night wandering about in the sparsely wooded country near the village and in the morning, when we had got our bearings from the sun, we made for the south. We could hear shots and the barking of dogs from our pursuers, who were getting close. We decided to split up and try different routes through the forest. I found myself with a Chechen called Vakha Chadaev.

Totally exhausted because we had not stopped for a rest, we wandered into some taiga[1] village consisting of perhaps twenty or so wooden houses. In the very first hut a middle-aged woman took us in. We told her everything and she fed us and put us to bed. The next morning she warned us not to show ourselves in the village until we had decided where we would go next. The woman herself went off to work. She had a daughter who also worked and an eleven-year-old son. Her husband had been arrested in 1937 and had died in a camp. Their family was one of many which had been deported as a kulak family from Northern Kazakhstan in 1930. Here in this taiga village they had their own small-holding: hens, pigs, cows and a vegetable garden. We lived with this family for about three weeks. Although the woman had warned us not to go out, one day in her absence we decided to saw up all the firewood there was near the house and give her a pleasant surprise. When the family gathered that evening, the mother and daughter took us to task, saying that we must have been seen by the neighbours. Although there was some member of every family who had been arrested, the local population was only too glad to give information about fugitives for the reward.

After this incident we decided to move on at dawn. The woman explained to us where the railway was. It transpired that there were two: one went to Sverdlovsk and was about 100 kilometres away; the other was the Trans-Siberian which

[1] Siberian forest.

lay about 300 kilometres from where we were. We decided to make for the latter. The woman supplied us with rusks, salt and home-made butter, and saw us off from the house at four o'clock in the morning.

There was still not much snow and we moved at a leisurely pace, keeping clear of main roads. No sooner did it get light, however, than two guards in military uniform emerged from the forest and came straight towards us. Of course we had no papers, so they tied our hands and took us away. We walked for a long time and eventually came to some village. There they sat us on a sledge and brought us to Bogoslovsk. For some unknown reason we weren't beaten but were put at once in a punishment block. It was full of lads from Nizhnyaya Tura who had refused to work. After a few days in there I and the others were sent for transfer.

We arrived at a station called Karelino. We were admitted to the compound and put in a separate hut, divided into two dormitories. The hut was not far from the punishment block.

On the very first day, the governor of the commandant's camp[1] of camp section 7 of Sevurallag, one Bestuzhev, came into our hut. He was known thereafter simply as Makhno.[2] He said that the only kind of work they did there was lumberjacking, that we would be under heavy guard, so we might as well give up any thought of escape, 'or else I shall turn you into Kerch herring, which as you know are black and headless'.

Apart from our batch, all the prisoners in the camp had been sentenced under the political articles. Many of the work teams were formed on a national basis from people living in different huts.[3] Thus there were three teams of Koreans (the Koreans

[1] The prison camp structure is roughly as follows. 'Main Administration of Camps' (Gulag) in Moscow. Subordinate to that of the 'Administrations', i.e. systems of camps divided into individual camp sections. The Commandant's Camp referred to here would probably be a small separate camp attached to one of these camp sections.
[2] Nestor Makhno, Anarchist leader in the Ukraine during the Civil War.
[3] Usually the opposite is the case, and members of a team share the same dormitory and hut, cf *One Day in the Life of Ivan Denisovich*.

were arrested initially in the Far East, and later their families were re-settled in Central Asia), German teams made up of Volga Germans and Germans who had lived in the Caucasian colonies of 'Luxemburg' and 'Elendorf'; Georgian teams (the team leader of one of them was Pyotr Yenukidze, the son of Abel Yenukidze),[1] the Mingrelians[2] by the way were in a separate team; there were teams from the Kuban composed of strapping Cossacks; Kabardinian,[3] Kazakh and Chechen teams. The rest were all sorts and conditions and were employed in the main on ancillary work. There was a small women's hut in the camp with about thirty inmates.

Today, after almost thirty years, I can still remember the jobs we did in the lumber camp. First the actual felling of the tree, followed by hauling it to the temporary[4] narrow-gauge railway, then the moving of the logs to the exchange. The 'exchange' was by the railway proper and amounted to a cordoned off working compound about a square kilometre in area. At the 'exchange', the full lengths of timber were stacked. Throughout the winter loads – large sledges stacked with timber – were sent down a sledge run improvised from spars. The logs were 6 metres 57 centimetres in length. They were then divided into shorter lengths; the shortest lengths of firewood 75 cms; ordinary firewood $1\frac{1}{2}$ metres; pit props from 1m. 10 cms to $1\frac{1}{2}$ metres. Aspen wood was used for matches and barrel staves; birch went for reels and bobbins, the blocks from which the stocks of guns were made, and the root went for ski blocks. Lengths from $5\frac{1}{2}$ to $6\frac{1}{2}$ metres were suitable for sawing into planks, 2·8 metre lengths would do as the blocks for railway sleepers.

To all intents and purposes our team had no team leader because not one of us would agree to accept the job – for the

---

[1] Former Secretary of the Central Executive Committee and a close colleague of Stalin's. He was expelled from the Party in 1935 and shot in December 1937.
[2] A Georgian ethnic group.
[3] A people of the North Caucasus.
[4] i.e. standing simply on sleepers without ballast.

rogues it would have been an infringement of their law to take the job and it was pointless and even dangerous to appoint someone from another team: he might have been killed, and this Makhno knew all too well.

For several days we went down to the exchange, but we did no work and sat by the campfire. They decided to send us into the forest to the timber slide some five kilometres from the 'exchange'. We were taken there under heavy guard. No one cared to mind the fire for the guards although the fire-minder didn't have to work. This came as no surprise to the guards. We carried the tree trunks without any sense of urgency and kept stopping to warm ourselves at the campfire. At about midday while the guards were having their lunch (we weren't supposed to have any lunch), we were left unsupervised. As I went up to a stack of firewood, I heard that our chaps had decided to take this chance to escape. There were ten of us. After conferring together, we decided that eight of us would go.

Two of us took lengths of timber and went back, and the rest of us split into two groups and ran off into the forest fanning out as we went. The snow was not very deep. Some thirty minutes later we heard two shots in succession; the guards' usual signal when there had been an escape. I was with a young thief known as Imp. About two hours later we came to the edge of the forest. To reach the next area of forest, we had to cross an open space, a field three kilometres across. When we had already covered the greater part of the distance and had only another three hundred metres to cross to reach the forest, horsemen appeared behind us at the far edge of the field. They caught up with us. They were guards from our camp with Bestuzhev the governor in charge. There was no point in resisting. We were tied up and beaten with beech staves and whips and then each of us had ropes attached to his arms and was pulled through the snow behind the horses. Sometimes the horses went into a trot and we were dragged after them. It was not a 'journey' one looks back on with any pleasure. At any moment we could have bashed our heads against a tree stump, but in fact nothing terrible did happen. We were dragged into the compound, beaten up again and carried off to the punishment block (we were no longer capable of walking). I spent a month in the punishment block. For the first six days I couldn't even get up to use the slop pail. My cell mates lifted me up. My body was a mass of aches, but fortunately there were no broken bones so nature took its course and all my injuries healed. The other escapees like us had been caught and were in the neighbouring cells. This was my last escape.

A month later I emerged from the punishment block. They forced us to go out to work, but we were still refusing actually to do anything, so we took with us our 300-gramme punishment ration of bread and kilka,[1] which was supplied in unlimited quantities. We would arrive at the exchange, light a campfire, sit down and toast bread and kilka on sticks. When the foreman, who was not a prisoner, came up to us, we would smile and say that we hadn't finished having our lunch. And so the working day went by. Sometimes, our governor Makhno came galloping up to us on horseback. We jumped up and fled from the campfire in all directions among the piles of wood, where a horse couldn't pass and teased Bestuzhev: 'Count Bestuzhev![2] Makhno! We'll fuck you!' For all these tricks of ours we landed in the punishment block at regular intervals.

In the depth of winter we took up robbery. A high road passed through the exchange, and the free population's sledges with their loads were obliged to use it – there was no other road. We would wait for a train of sledges –two or three of them – and when it reached the middle of the exchange, we would leap out from both sides armed with axes and take everything that interested us, largely food, and then bless the travellers on their way. I remember once we got hold of a carcass of meat, which we afterwards roasted over our campfire. There were other occasions when we dragged away whole sacks of flour, dried peas, and sugar, and hid them all in the wood stacks in specially

---

[1] A small (and exceedingly revolting) fish.
[2] Russian history has a number of eminent Bestuzhevs, among whom there were counts.

constructed hiding places. It was impossible for anyone else to find these stolen goods.

On one occasion when we didn't fancy going to work, we were forcibly herded towards the guardhouse. There the pink-cheeked Makhno was waiting for us. He was holding a large hump-backed salmon by the tail. Infuriated by our behaviour, he took a swing with his hump-backed salmon and dealt one of our team a heavy blow. The lad fell. In protest against this act of lawlessness we all lay down in the snow. The warders were obliged to carry us to the punishment block. Once we were there, all twelve of us in the one cell decided to set fire to it. The punishment block was built of wood. We broke off a small bit of wood, plaited a wick from some cotton wool we pulled out of the lining of a padded jacket, and by the age-old method of twirling the cotton wool and rubbing it against the bit of board, we made fire. We then chipped little pieces from the planks and lit a fire in one corner, after which we all lay down on the floor. The punishment block began to burn and the smoke almost choked us. The staff came running up and started to put out the fire without first releasing us from the cell. Water from the hose not only put out the fire, but flooded all the cells as well, which led to everyone being let out of the punishment block apart from people in our cell. We were split up into groups of three and put into separate cells and we were frozen stiff. It was freezing very hard outside and our clothing soon had a film of ice on it. We drummed on the floor to be let out of the punishment block and also to try and keep our circulation going, but no one paid any heed to us. Late that night one of the chaps had a bout of ulcer trouble. We began to bawl and demand that a doctor be sent. The lad was spitting blood. We went on knocking until morning came.

When the prisoners had gone off to work, the door was opened and we were allowed to go to the doctor. We took our friend by the arm and off we went. We walked like wooden dolls, for our legs were frozen quite stiff. Thus we reached the sick bay. The guard took our friend into the doctor's room and we were left waiting in the entrance hall. The guard quickly re-emerged and said that he had been put in hospital and we were to go back to the punishment block. We started bawling that we too needed medical attention. The guard cursed and ordered us to obey him. His shouting caused the doctor to come out and ignoring the guard completely he asked: 'And what's the matter with you?'

'We've got frostbite in our feet.'

He invited us to go into his surgery and told us to get undressed. He took a seat at the table and wrote down our surnames. When I said mine, he seemed to give an involuntary start and looked at me very closely. I had difficulty in pulling off one of my 'bakhila'.[1] When I did so I saw that my foot had turned quite blue. The same thing had happened to my friends. The doctor wrote something on a piece of paper and handed it to the guard. The guard read it and said the governor's instructions were that we had to stay in the punishment block. The doctor went to the telephone and made a call: 'Citizen warden, I have here at the surgery two prisoners with third degree frostbite in their feet. They must be let out of the punishment block for treatment; I, as a doctor, shall withdraw my services if my demands are not complied with.'

I don't know what answer the warden gave, but the doctor handed the receiver to the guard and we heard him reply: 'Very good sir.' Turning to the doctor he said: 'Give me a paper to say that they need treatment.' The doctor wrote out the appropriate paper and gave it to the guard. The guard left and we were alone with the doctor. He examined our feet very carefully and summoned a nurse who put on poultices for us. We went back to the hut and next morning were put in the sick quarters. In the sick quarters after he had done his rounds, the doctor invited me into the room where he lived. He asked me: 'Are you the son of the Yakir?' I said that I was.

'So I thought. Your feet are in a very bad way, but I'll try to do what I can. As long as I'm here you must never refuse to work. You'd do better to come to the sick bay beforehand. And a word of general advice. Imagine that you're part of an expedi-

[1] Camp issue padded socks.

tion which is studying human mores. Try to grasp the meaning of people's actions, observe and try to make sense of it all.'

This became my credo in camp life and the doctor Sergei Fyodorovich Preobrazhensky, became my spiritual father...

Sergei Fyodorovich was a palaeontologist by profession. He was the son of the rector of a religious seminary and at nineteen, during the Civil War, had joined the Red Army as a medical orderly. His elder brother, Pyotr Fyodorovich Preobrazhensky, was a most eminent Soviet specialist in ancient history. In 1937 the three Preobrazhensky brothers and the husbands of their two sisters were arrested. They were all tried at the same time under the same indictment and declared to belong to a 'monarchist organisation'. They collected ten years each and set out for various camps. When Pyotr Fyodorovich's wife came to see him in Onelag,[1] he said to her as they were saying goodbye, 'We shall all die in this mincing machine. The only one to survive will be Sergei. Since he was a child he's known how to approach life philosophically.' This prophecy came true.

After he had been set free, Sergei Fyodorovich worked in an institute of palaeontology. Despite bad health, even at the age of sixty he accompanied his students on expeditions, enjoyed life and everybody was very fond of him.

In 1957 Sergei Fyodorovich got a document of rehabilitation from Kazan, where he and his relations had been tried many years before. The document said: 'Sergei Fyodorovich Preobrazhensky has been posthumously rehabilitated.' The effect on him was disastrous; he was already paralysed and only lived for two more years.

I was in the hospital for one and a half months. My toes recovered and there was no need to amputate. I just lost the nails from my big toes. Sergei Fyodorovich and I chatted together a lot and I listened to him with great attention. Some good came of our meetings, for I began to educate myself. I read the books sent to Sergei Fyodorovich with avidity.

Spring came and I fell ill with pneumonia. When I was be-

[1] Onezhsky lager, a system of camps near lake Onega.

ginning to get better, I was called for transfer. Sergei Fyodorovich said that he would do everything he could to prevent my transfer. He gave me injections which sent up my temperature. The camp authorities decided not to transfer me while I was so ill. Mischa Medved left in the batch I should have gone in. As I found out later, they went to the Kolyma. His fate is unknown to me. There were rumours of the boat having foundered with the prisoners on board. I never heard any more of Mischa Medved.

The days rolled on. An enormous batch of prisoners came to the camp. It included Chechens, Ingushi and others. They were very 'rich'. They had huge supplies of food – dried mutton, pork fat, dried fruits. Our boys spent a whole two weeks gutting their kitbags, and there was feasting in our hut.

From April onwards, after the TASS denial of troops having been moved from eastern areas of the Soviet Union to the west had appeared in the papers, the imminence of war was a constant subject of conversation in the camp. After the famous TASS denial of 14 June,[1] however, Gottlieb Eduardovich Kurtz, a German teacher who was a foreman in the camp, stated on the basis of this information alone, that war would break out within a week.

On 22 June, no working parties went out. By the evening, rumours began to seep through into the camp that the war had begun. On 23 June they began to summon us for transfer, a hut at a time. For the most part it was Article 58-ers that were called. We were searched carefully, herded towards the guardhouse where a large escort including handlers with their dogs were standing. The massive batch of prisoners was lined up in sevens, and to the accompaniment of barking dogs we were marshalled down the road towards the forest. After walking through the forest for about eight kilometres, we saw the compound, a lumber camp called Malaya Kosalmanka, which had been empty for a year. Before we were admitted to the compound, the governor addressed us: 'Due to the fact that the

[1] This was an official denial that there was any truth in stories of an impending German attack on the Soviet Union.

fascist invaders have attacked the Soviet Union, I have to inform you of new camp regulations. Inside the compound you are not to assemble in groups of more than two persons. For breaking this regulation you will be put in the punishment block. Refusal to work and likewise an escape, will be classified under Article 58-14 (counter-revolutionary sabotage) and the culprits will be shot. Maximum ration if work quotas are fulfilled at 110% will be 625 grammes of bread, if only at 100% – 525; the punishment ration will be 275.'

This last statement gave the lie to the old camp proverb: 'The sun will still be in front wherever they chase you and you'll get 300 grammes of bread.'

After searching us once more, we were let into the compound and allocated to different huts. No bedding had been brought so we had to sleep on bare boards. For the first two days we got no midday meal and we decided that they hadn't had time to bring in any provisions, but in fact we lived on bread alone for a month and a half.

All the trees in the immediate area of the camp had long since been felled and the teams had to walk more than ten kilometres to their place of work. The absence of hot food, reduced bread ration, ten kilometre walks to work, and an eleven-hour working day, which did not include the time taken walking to and from work, all led to the prisoners being on their last legs by the end of the first two months of the war. All lags who had been convicted under Article 58 were removed from privileged jobs as book-keepers, store-keepers, doctors, etc. Sergei Fyodorovich also worked in the forest now.

At the beginning of August, our group of teams was again transferred to another camp, Bolshaya Kosalmanka, close to the railway. Beside it was a women's compound and a huge exchange, where both men and women worked. To get to work we had to cover five to seven kilometres. I was put in a brigade of teenagers and began working at the exchange. At that period a neighbouring collective farm used to let its herds of goats and rams out to graze there. We decided to supplement our diet. This we did by catching some animal, dealing with it and stewing the meat in a bucket. The prey was shared out equally. Unbearable hunger caused us to steal the collective farm stock. When they found they were seventy goats and rams short, the collective farm stopped letting its stock roam around the exchange.

Autumn set in. Urgent felling of selected trees began. On the whole birch trees were selected and sawn up for ski blocks and rifle stocks and side pieces. The war department gave an additional 100 grammes of bread and a packet of makhorka per week to prisoners fulfilling quotas in these areas. Even though by this time we had started getting thin soup and a little kasha, nothing made much difference to the starving lags. No one fulfilled the quota. Georgians and men from the Kuban, who had formerly looked like epic heroes, had become bags of bones which scarcely moved. If before the war it had taken four men until lunch time to load a flat car with building timber, it now took a hundred men the whole day to do the same work. People were dying at work and in the compound. On all the medical records it said 'AD2' (dystrophy) and 'BBO' (Oedema caused by albumen deficiency).

Winter came. One day we woke up and saw a large prison train standing near the compound. This was the usual way a batch of prisoners was delivered. No one, however, was being unloaded. The guards were dashing about the compound, looking for people who knew how to drive horses. Eventually they got together a team and took them under guard to the stables. There the guards had them harness up either sledges or drags. This cavalcade was driven up to the prison train. They began opening the doors. People were lying in the carriages. The batch had come from BBK. The women, who were from Medvezhia Gora, were still mobile, the men could not walk. In every truck load of forty men, there were five or six corpses. Somewhere near Cherepovets the staff carriage had been bombed and all the lags' dossiers had been blown to bits, so that the new arrivals formally speaking had no sentence and they themselves wrote down their own basic data. They had been in transit for about two months. At first they had been issued with a mug of flour each day, but for the last ten days they hadn't had anything to eat at all. When people had cried out for help while the train was standing in stations, the guards had fired at the windows, and told people they had fascist traitors on board. The men were brought to the camp by horse transport. Those that were still alive came to the compound, the dead were taken to the camp cemetery. I happened to be in a team digging graves there at that time. The digging was quite primitive. We lit large fires, then raked out the thawed earth. Into the large holes thus formed we bundled fifteen or twenty bodies. Old traditions were still observed. Each dead man had a wooden tag fastened to his leg with his number branded on it.

Once a train of evacuees stopped not far from our exchange. It was some plant being moved from the Ukraine. Side by side on the cars stood machine tools and hastily constructed small houses, in which people were huddled. We got into conversation with them. They threw us bread, tobacco and sugar. The evacuees asked us in surprise, 'And who are you then?'

'Prisoners.'

'Are you really? All ours were set free before the Germans came.'

One of our number, the former inmate of a death cell, quipped ironically: 'Well, perhaps when the Germans get as far as here, they'll set us free too.'

As I discovered later the evacuees' information was not quite accurate. I know from reliable sources that when the Germans reached Byelorussia, for example, Soviet guards shot political prisoners on the spot, both in the camps and in the prisons. That was what happened in Minsk.

At the end of October, Sergei Fyodorovich's wife came to see him. No meeting was granted, but for a consideration, the senior warder made it possible for him to see her at the exchange during working hours. By this time Sergei Fyodorovich looked like a skeleton held together with skin and the fifteen kilogrammes of food that his wife had brought were but a drop in the ocean. He returned from the meeting completely crushed.

His wife had told him about the events of 16 October in Moscow. This was a dreadful day for Moscow. The rumour got about that Stalin and other members of the government had left the city. All who could then rushed to the stations or set off on foot along the highways. The air above the Lubyanka at that time was full of the ash of burnt paper. There was looting of shops and warehouses.

The parcel was quickly eaten and once again the days were hungry. For a long time we had no sugar, meat or fats. Yet another misfortune overtook us however: the store ran out of salt. For more than a month the camp lived without salt and people would give three bread rations of 675 grammes for a matchbox full of salt. The saltless diet cut people down in yet greater numbers.

THE 'SALT' STORY

In the spring of 1942 in the commandant's camp of Karelino, in Sevurallag, the salt ran out. This was a noticeable addition to all our other misfortunes. Many people did not know what to do with themselves. The saltless bread and the batter made from grated flour they were fed on, made them sick. Although everybody was incredibly hungry, a matchbox full of salt at the start fetched 100 grammes of bread and a month later, the maximum ration, 675 grammes. The prisoners' bodies, which were already exhausted, grew yet weaker for lack of salt. The whole camp reminded one of Dante's purgatory, except that the shades moved at a speed ten times slower than that of Dante's shades. One flat car of building timber which four men had loaded in three hours before the war, now took 200 men ten hours to load. There were ninety of them to a rope trying to get a trunk rolling with the weight of their emaciated bodies. 'One, two, three, up!' This refrain sounded now as though it were coming from beneath the ground.

One morning a train of flat cars stopped on the through line. On them there was something white, like salt. People rushed towards the train. The soldiers on the watch towers fired several times into the air. They weren't afraid of anyone running away, because they knew no one had the stomach for running anywhere. They just fired the shots for form's sake. The prisoners tasted the white crystals, which seemed to have a salty taste and to a man they stuffed their pockets and hats and any other bits of rag they had with this 'salt'. That night people were taken to the hospital with acute vomiting. About 300 men died. The crystals were saltpetre.

In December, I had a stroke of luck. A former planner called Zhitomirsky fixed me a job as assistant orderly in the hut of the loading team. The very next day this team was dispatched to the neighbouring camp of Obzhig. Their things remained in the hut and the orderly, a robust, pock-marked rogue called Mischka, whose nickname was the Stallion, and I, were left looking after them. Soon afterwards he and I commenced systematic pilfering of the clothes store. It was not far from our hut and was guarded at night by Estonians, from the domestic staff.[1]

At the beginning of 1941 there had been wholesale deportations from all the Baltic republics. NKVD special purposes detachments had, on the basis of previously compiled lists, arrested people from bourgeois families: small shop-keepers, white-collar workers, former nobles, former policemen. Each was allowed to take with him sixteen kilogrammes of luggage, including food. Families were split up. Men and women were deported separately sixty to a box car. From what the arrivals said twelve such trains had left Riga and about the same number had come from Tallin and Vilnius. By the beginning of the war, almost all these trains had got to the Gorky-Perm area and by 1 July, they began to arrive in the camps of the Urals and Northern Kazakhstan. The occupants had been very badly fed en route and when the trains were unloaded, people were scarcely able to walk out of the cars.

Two trains from Riga and one each from Tallin and Vilnius came to us in Camp 7 of Sevurallag. All the new arrivals were by our standards dressed like 'kings': fine suits, shoes, over-

[1] Domestic staff, as opposed to the work force. Prisoners who worked in the running of the camp.

coats. Their appearance was very quickly taken care of. They were sold bags of sugar which had sugar on the top and fine sand from the river underneath. The Balts were a very trusting lot who were not used to being 'conned'. A month later they were walking about in third-hand camp uniforms, and trying to find something to eat among the rubbish. I remember the case of the secretary of the President of Lithuania who was so weak that he couldn't climb out of a dustbin into which he had clambered to get some rotten fish heads.

In October the OSO decision was announced to all the Balts: each of them got ten years. They were all accused of the same thing: counter-revolutionary activity. I didn't have much occasion to talk to them, but I do remember that they looked down on the Russians for their lack of culture and beggarly mode of life. This matter of culture is a vexed question. Not only the Balts, but many western intellectuals who found themselves in the camps turned out to be far more badly educated than representatives of the Russian intelligentsia.

As it was very cold, the Estonians who were guarding the store, dashed into the office every few minutes to warm themselves up. Mischka took an impression from the lock and made a key; when the watchmen went to the office, we snipped out, unfastened the lock and one of us slipped into the store. The other one shut him in and fifteen minutes or so later, when the watchmen once again departed, the door was opened and the things carried out. In the main we tried to take padded jackets, felt boots, sheets, anything new that hadn't been issued before. We then packed everything into sacks and took it to the guardhouse. The guard there settled with us in bread, meat, makhorka and sugar. The payment was pathetically small: for two new padded jackets, a pair of felt boots and three sheets, he offered a loaf of bread, half a kilogramme of meat, two packets of makhorka and five large lumps of sugar. On one occasion he brought up some neat spirit. When the storekeepers declared their losses, they were sacked. We carried on like this for two months.

Occasionally women would come into our compound to see the doctor. On the whole they were 'lady thieves'. Mischka used to get involved in affairs with them, but I kept out of their way.

I helped Sergei Fyodorovich as best as I could, because I was in a much more advantageous position than he. He had to go several kilometres into the forest, but as he could hardly walk, there was no question of him doing any sawing. He busied himself 'treating' the tree-trunks: he had two little bottles of chemicals with which he removed the tally marks and then handed in these trunks as if he'd sawn them up himself. One had to fulfil at least twenty per cent of the quota in order to get the 450 grammes 'basic' ration.

Towards the spring I was transferred to the commandant's camp, Karelino. The situation there was still worse: out of 2,000 men there were only a hundred or so working. Every day between ten and twenty men died. The living were falling apart in front of your eyes.

The whole winter we were tormented by lice. No amount of roasting or bathing would get rid of them. We rid ourselves of them by taking off our shirts and underpants and holding them over a red hot stove. Three and four times each day we would roast up to a hundred of these fat 'snipes'. We were scratching from morning till night; it was enough to drive you mad.

Right at the very beginning of the war, most people convicted under Article 58 applied for active service, but received no answer. Prisoners who had served five years' sentences were kept on in the camps under the rubrics 'awaiting special instructions' or 'until the end of the war'. Their terms ended for the most part in 1942, but they stayed in prison until 1948.

One French communist wrote several applications for active service. He received no reply and was very far gone. One day on the way to work, he made a run to one side. All this happened in full view of the whole team. The guard fired twice and wounded him in both legs. In the hospital he went on hunger strike, but no one made any attempt to feed him and on the ninth day he died.

In the spring of 1942, Volga Germans were brought to fill the unoccupied compounds of our camp, which had become empty on account of the enormous number of deaths. Sometimes they worked with us at the exchange. They told us how they had been deported without explanation. Military units of the MVD drove them en masse from their homes, loaded them on to lorries and took them to the railway, where they were put on to trains. All their stock was left unattended and the soldiers took pot-shots at the animals for fun. An enormous number of animals simply perished.

At the commandant's camp I found a horrific situation. All the huts apart from one had been turned into sick quarters. The hundred or so people who could still go to work became blind as soon as night fell. This was caused by a vitamin deficiency, which ordinary folk call 'Chicken's blindness'. I didn't suffer from this, but so as not to stand out from the others I simulated blindness. All evening work, which in the main was loading railway waggons, was halted. Even the camp authorities, who before this had taken no notice of the doctors, did not dare to drive blind men out into the night. A little later the camp authorities began to issue a hundred grammes of sheep's liver per head per day. In a few days most people could once again see normally.

In July 1942, they delivered some mouldy rye flour to the camp. All teams were hurriedly sent to unload it. Many ate the flour raw and then later in the camp it was used to make a kind of batter. Salt was short and this batter tasted awful, but you could eat as much of it as your belly would hold. The survivors began to look better, and fill out like dough rising with the yeast. It was only a seeming recovery, however. People were still suffering from oedema and many were still dying. Once they brought some beetroot and issued one beetroot per person. Everybody's face and body turned red.

At that time, as a result of rumours that had reached the capital, a commission from Moscow came to check Sevurallag. Many lags were sent for and asked about the diet and discipline during the first year of the war. The commission was at work for about a month. All the wardens of the camps, senior warders, and escort commanders, were arrested. They were tried in

August and many lags gave evidence. The administration was charged with not observing the law, beating up prisoners, shooting them, cutting rations, etc. They were all sentenced to various terms of imprisonment qualified by the phrase already widespread at the time 'replaced by active service'.

The newly-arrived 'brass' was composed for the most part of wounded veterans, and life in the camp became noticeably easier. The guards and the warders spoke to us and the food improved a bit. They began to give sprouting peas to people suffering from scurvy. For the first time, the OPP (the Prophylactic and Recuperating Centres) were set up. The people in our camp who were furthest gone were put in the OPP for two months. Lags in the OPP did not work and were fed reasonably well: 800 grammes of bread, soup, kasha twice a day, 20 grammes of sugar, 20 grammes of butter and 100 grammes of meat or fish. They were also issued with 20 grammes of fish oil and a tablespoonful of nicotic acid, twice daily. In the dining-hall there also appeared barrels of an infusion made from pine needles, which no one before had realised could be used as a treatment for scurvy.

A woman doctor who was a graduate of the Moscow Medical Institute and not a prisoner, knowing that I had only two months to go to the end of my term, put me in the OPP, although I was in a reasonable state of health. I did not think they would set me free, as they were hanging on to everybody else. Seven days before the end of my term I was discharged from the OPP. To avoid tormenting myself during those last days I asked for some luminal in the sick bay; and in the morning, after I'd eaten my bread ration, I took it with hot water, and slept for the whole day. Nobody woke me up to go to work. The day of freedom came. Still half asleep I wandered into the transfer registry, where I was calmly told that I would be detained pending special instructions. I was warned that I would have to go to work on the following day.

That same day Sergei Fyodorovich arrived in a batch of prisoners from Bolshaya Kosalmanka. The next day we went out to the forest working area. We went deep into the trees and talked for a long time sitting by a campfire. I put forward various ideas: an escape, a hunger strike, a further request to be sent on active service, or killing some highly unpopular boss. Sergei Fyodorovich rejected all these suggestions. He reminded me that I wasn't the only one, and that at that moment no one was being let out, and a hunger strike or an escape would lead to my being tried for counter-revolutionary sabotage. He told me that not long before at Bolshaya Kaselmanka several men had been shot for discussing the encirclement of our troops near Kharkov in the spring of 1942. We spent several days by the fire doing nothing. The team leader apparently told the authorities and we were transferred to the 'exchange'. At the 'exchange' there was nowhere where one could get out of the way, and we had at least to make a show of taking part in loading railway waggons. Trainloads of wounded kept passing; they kept us supplied with makhorka and sometimes even gave us bread and sugar.

A month passed and I was suddenly summoned for transfer. I wasn't told where I was going and my friends and I hazarded all sorts of guesses. We supposed that they wanted to remove me and settle accounts with me for my being one of the chief witnesses in the case against the camp administration. That evening I was put on board a passing Stolypin and travelled northwards. A few hours later we arrived at the station of Sosva, where the administration of Sevurallag was.

The punishment camp was there too. To judge from what people said about it, there weren't many worse camps, and I decided that I was being sent there. The rule of law was absent there to such an extent that the administration didn't even enter the compound but threw the bread over the fence. Rogues' anarchy ruled the roost and they would most likely have killed even an ordinary muzhik if he had not grovelled before them.

Contrary to my suppositions, however, I was put in the central camp prison, where I stayed for about ten days. One evening I was sent for and taken I know not where. One guard walked in front of me and another behind. We walked along a narrow path and all the time I thought I was about to be shot.

After walking about two kilometres we came to a large single-storey wooden house with electric lighting. We entered the building and went up to one of the doors. Written on it was 'Chief of the Operational Chekist Branch of Sevurallag, Colonel Petrov'. The door opened wide, I went in and the guard remained outside.

The room was large. In it was a desk, a sofa and bookshelves. At the desk sat a grey-haired colonel and beside him two women. 'How do you do? Sit down,' said the colonel, pointing to an armchair, and then turning to the women. 'Well you've seen him, now you can go.'

The women went out leaving the two of us together. The colonel said: 'So this is what you're like. I thought you'd be older-looking and a bit bigger. Don't you forget that I know all about you. I think that at bottom you're a Soviet man and will do all you can to redeem your father's guilt.'

'I don't know what my father's guilt is. In the camp I've been told by many people that he did nothing wrong.'

'Well, we won't go into that now. He was convicted as a traitor and you have to prove that you're a real Soviet man.'

'I have several times volunteered for active service and would gladly give my life for my country.'

The colonel pressed a button and a girl entered the room with a tray. On it was a beefsteak, fried potatoes, two pieces of bread and sausage and a decanter of wine.

'Now first you have something to eat and then you and I will have a talk,' said the colonel, and locking the safe and the drawers of his desk, he left the room.

I wavered for a moment before deciding to dispose of the grub. The wine was rather weak. The meat and the sausage were very tasty. When I had eaten everything I felt like a smoke. At that moment, just as it happens in fairy tales, the colonel reappeared and without even waiting for me to ask, offered me a packet of 'Kazbek'. He then said: 'Tomorrow you'll be sent back to Camp 7. We have decided to set you free. You are not to speak of this to anyone in the camp. Before long you'll be sent to Sverdlovsk where arrangements will be made for you to work and to study. I think you will repay our confidence.'

I was taken away and the next day arrived safely at Karelino station. I told the whole story to Sergei Fyodorovich. For a long time he was silent and then he said: 'Well, my son, from now on you'll be dancing on a knife edge. Just you see you don't slip or else that knife will be plunged straight into your side. Playing games with those gentlemen is very dangerous.'

Five days later they sent for me to set me free. I was given a loaf of bread and two herrings and I came out of the compound. A stranger in mufti saw me to the administration. In the security officer's office, I was allowed to change into a new camp uniform, given two lumps of sugar and a tin of meat. We set off by the evening train, travelling in a separate compartment and next morning we arrived in Sverdlovsk. I was taken by car to the regional administration of the NKVD. There a man in mufti saw me and asked me to sign an undertaking not to leave Sverdlovsk. He told me that I would be found a place in the hostel of the Polytechnic and accepted as a student. He warned me that people I knew like Svetlana Tukhachevskaya, Victoria Gamarnik and Gizi Steinbruck were living in the town, that I would be under surveillance and that for divulging information about the camps I would be prosecuted under Article 121 of the Criminal Code. He also warned me that they would want to see me and talk with me at regular intervals. He then sent for a man who drove me to the hostel of the Higher Technical Institute complex.

1971

Appendices

APPENDIX 1

The Execution of Pyotr Yakir's Father

by Robert Conquest

In 1937 Army Commander First Class Ion Yakir was a powerful and respected figure – the only military man proper who was also a full member of the Central Committee of the Communist Party. He was then forty-one.

Yakir was the son of a small Jewish pharmacist in Kishinev. When only twenty-one, he organised a Bolshevik group in the Ukraine, then the scene of continuous fighting between a variety of contenders for power. Within three years he had risen to command the 'Fastov Army Groups' in the war against Poland. In 1926 he was appointed to command the key Ukrainian (later Kiev) Military District – by far the largest army outside the Far East – a post which he held at the time of his arrest.

Stalin's purge of the Red Army, which very nearly led to Hitler winning the war in 1941, had started in August 1936, when a friend of Army Commander Yakir's, Divisional Commander Dmitri Shmidt, was arrested and, following him, another senior officer, Corps Commander Putna, military attaché in London. They were implicated at the notorious Zinoviev show trial that month, when one of the accused spoke even more ominously of a whole 'Trotskyite group of military men'.

Shmidt, after defending himself for some time, broke down under interrogation (his interrogators included the notorious Z. M. Ushakov whose speciality was breaking people's ribs). His confession, of planning to raise his tank unit in revolt for Trotskyite purposes, then seems to have been circulated to senior officers. Yakir, determined to check the charges, insisted on seeing Shmidt in jail. Shmidt, though now pale and listless and quite unlike his usual self – reminding Yakir of a being from another planet – all the same repudiated his confession when they met. Yakir was not allowed to question him on details, but had him write a note to Voroshilov declaring his innocence. Yakir went back to Kiev, glad to have cleared up the misunderstanding. But soon afterwards Voroshilov rang up to say that on the very next day Shmidt had reaffirmed his confessions.

Meanwhile Stalin had set in motion one of the most extraordinary intrigues of the period, the facts of which have only recently been confirmed from Soviet sources. Starting in December 1936, the Foreign Department of the NKVD began manoeuvres to compromise the generals by inventing contacts between them and the German High Command. Approaches were made to the Nazi Sicherheitsdienst (SD), and information was got to the head of the latter, Heydrich, that the Soviet army leaders were conspiring with the German General Staff. The SD realised that this was untrue, but took the opportunity to provide 'confirmation', with a view to helping destroy the Russian military leadership. First, the Germans 'leaked' to President Beneš of Czechoslovakia their supposed reliance on the Soviet generals. Beneš reported this to Stalin, who thus had 'evidence'. In March 1937 the Germans forged a dossier confirming these acts of military treason by documents allegedly signed by Tukhachevsky and others. This was passed direct to the NKVD and was in Stalin's hands by mid-May.

Over the winter Shmidt, Putna, Corps Commander Primakov and others had been worked on for further confessions incriminating Yakir and others. In January the second great show trial, of Pyatakov, Radek and others took place. After it Yakir was told of the last words of one of the accused, Yakov Livshits, Assistant People's Commissar of Communications: 'Why?'. Yakir commented that it was a good question, as the accused were clearly innocent. In fact, he saw the whole falsehood of the purge. At the end of February came the crucial 'February–March' plenum of the Central Committee, when the military members of that Committee, Yakir among them, are reported as opposing any further extensions of the purge. Stalin outmanoeuvred the opposition, secured the arrest of Bukharin and others, and from that moment on found himself in a position to launch totally indiscriminate mass arrests.

With the Army he at first proceeded carefully. In April various officers were arrested, including Yakir's brother-in-law, Corps Commander Garkavy. Yakir went to Stalin to complain and was told that evidence against Garkavy had been given by officers arrested earlier, but that if he were innocent he would be released.

11 May saw Army Commander Kork arrested. On 20 May Dmitri Shmidt was shot in secret without further ado. Over the following week general after general was arrested and real panic now gripped the officer corps. On the 26th, Marshal Tukhachevsky, on arriving at the backwoods Volga Command to which he had been transferred, was himself seized.

On 28 May, Yakir attended a conference at the Kiev military district at which the news of Tukhachevsky's arrest was officially, though confidentially, announced. One of the officers present reports

Yakir, normally a cheerful man, as plunged in gloom. The next day Voroshilov ordered him to come to Moscow for a meeting of the Military Revolutionary Soviet. Yakir offered to fly, but was ordered to take the train, on which (as Pyotr Yakir tells us here) he was arrested on the early morning of 31 May. He was bundled into a Black Maria and driven at high speed to Moscow. In the Lubyanka gaol his chevrons and medals were ripped off and he was put into a solitary cell.

He at once wrote to the Politburo demanding immediate release or a meeting with Stalin. Instead he was severely interrogated and was told that the 'whole Yakir nest' had been arrested. Two hundred officers were seized in Kiev. Among Yakir's 'nest' was Army Commissar Yan Berzin who, under the pseudonym 'Gorev' had been effective Commander-in-Chief of the Spanish Republican Army in the Battle of Madrid, and was to be shot in July 1938.

From his cell Yakir sent a letter to Stalin assuring him of his complete innocence.

He wrote: '. . . My entire conscious life has been spent working selflessly and honestly in full view of the Party and its leaders. . . . Every word I say is honest, and I shall die with words of love for you, the Party, and the country, with boundless faith in the victory of Communism.'

Stalin wrote on this letter: 'Scoundrel and prostitute.' Voroshilov added: 'A perfectly accurate description.' Molotov put his name to this and Kaganovich appended: 'For the traitor, scum and (next comes a scurrilous, obscene word) one punishment – the death sentence.'

At the meeting of the Supreme Military Council, summons to which had been the pretext of Yakir's call to Moscow, the only item on the agenda was 'the exposure of the counter-revolutionary military-fascist organisation'. Stalin personally demanded the death penalty for all the arrested. On 11 June, in the first public statement to be made on the case, it was announced that they were accused of 'breach of military duty and oath of allegiance, treason to their country, treason against the peoples of the USSR, and treason against the Workers' and Peasants' Red Army'. (A report by Voroshilov published on 15 June added, 'preparing the assassination of leaders of the party and government', as well as espionage'.)

The trial too took place on 11 June. No full account of it has ever been published. Pyotr Yakir in this book gives some details which had not previously been registered. Other accounts published in the USSR confirm that Yakir was personally accused of having been recruited by the German Secret Service while on a visit to Berlin and that he indignantly repudiated the charge.

On 12 June it was announced that all the accused had been executed.

Khrushchev tells us that 'When Yakir was shot he exclaimed: "Long live the Party, long live Stalin!" . . . When Stalin was told how Yakir had behaved before his death, he cursed Yakir.' We know Yakir had thought of his family; and it was clearly not in their interests for him to utter words of defiance or abuse. He had made a last appeal for them. Before he was shot, he sent Voroshilov this letter:

'To K. Ye. Voroshilov. I ask you, in memory of my many years of honest service in the Red Army in the past, to give instructions that my family, helpless and quite innocent, shall be looked after and given assistance. I have addressed the same plea to N. I. Yezhov. Yakir.' On this Voroshilov minuted, 'In general I doubt the dishonesty of a dishonest person.'

Pyotr Yakir had told us elsewhere that his father's grave was one of several desecrated on Stalin's orders.

It has not been possible to trace the fate of his mother. The wives of others shot with Ion Yakir were executed in 1941, after four years in the camps.

The accused of the June 1937 trial were certainly innocent, and they have long since been rehabilitated in the USSR. Their execution marked the beginning of a vast purge of the army, which led to the arrest of over 30,000 officers. Among those executed were 3 of the 5 marshals, 14 of the 16 Army Commanders, all 8 of the Admirals, 60 of the 67 Corps Commanders, 136 of the 199 Divisional Commanders. For this virtual decapitation of the Red Army, Russia had to pay in 1941–2 with huge losses in territory and men, when the Nazis struck.

Yet the purge in the Army was only part of the vaster purge, of whose nature Pyotr Yakir gives us so many insights in this book.

APPENDIX 2

Article 58 of the Criminal Code of the RSFR

(*repealed December 1959*)

Special Section: Chapter 1

1. Counter-Revolutionary Crimes

Art. 58–1. Any act designed to overthrow, undermine or weaken the authority of the workers' and peasants' Soviets and the workers' and peasants' government of the Union of Soviet Socialist Republics, of the Union and Autonomous Republics, elected by the Soviets on the basis of the Constitution of the USSR and the Constitutions of the Union Republics or designed to undermine or weaken the external security of the USSR and of the basic economic, political and national achievements of the proletarian revolution, is deemed to be a counter-revolutionary act.

In view of the international solidarity of the interests of all the toilers, such acts are also regarded as counter-revolutionary when they are directed against any other Workers' State, even though not forming part of the USSR.

Art. 58–1a. Treason against the homeland, i.e. acts committed by citizens of the USSR to the detriment of the military strength of the USSR, its State independence, or the inviolability of its territory, such as: espionage, betrayal of a military or State secret, desertion to the enemy, flight abroad by land or air are punishable: by the supreme measure of criminal punishment – death by shooting and the confiscation of all property; in extenuating circumstances – by deprivation of liberty for a period of ten years and the confiscation of all property.

Art. 58–1b. These same crimes, if committed by military personnel, are punishable by the supreme measure of criminal punishment – death by shooting and confiscation of all property.

Art. 58–1c. In the event of flight abroad by land or air of a member of the armed forces, the adult members of his family, if they in any way assisted the preparation of the commission of this act of treason, or even if they knew of it but failed to report it to the authorities, are to be punished: by deprivation of liberty for a period of from five to ten years and confiscation of all property.

The remaining adult members of the traitor's family, and those living with him or dependent on him at the time of the commission of the crime are liable to deprivation of their electoral rights and to exile to the remote areas of Siberia for a period of five years.

Art. 58–1d. Failure on the part of a member of the armed forces to report preparations for or the commission of an act of treason entails:

> deprivation of liberty for ten years.

Failure on the part of other citizens (not members of the armed forces) to report is punished in accordance with Article 58–12.

Art. 58–2. Armed insurrection or incursion of armed bands into Soviet territory, with counter-revolutionary aims, the seizure of power at the centre or in the provinces with the same aims and, in particular, with the aim of forcibly separating from the USSR or from a separate Union Republic any part of its territory or of violating treaties concluded between the USSR and foreign States, entail:

> the supreme measure of social defence – death by shooting, or declaration as an enemy of the labouring masses, and the confiscation of property and deprivation of citizenship of the Union Republic and thereby of the USSR, and banishment beyond the frontiers of the USSR for ever; in extenuating circumstances a reduction of sentence is permitted to deprivation of liberty for a period of not less than three years and the confiscation of all or part of the property.

Art 58–3. Maintenance of relations for counter-revolutionary purposes with foreign States or with individual representatives of those States and also assistance, rendered by any means whatsoever, to a foreign State at war with the USSR or engaged in fighting the USSR by means of intervention or blockade entail:

> measures of social defence as indicated in Article 58–2 of the present Code.

Art. 58–4. The rendering of assistance, by any means whatsoever, to that section of the international bourgeoisie, which, not recognising the equal rights of the communist system which is coming to replace the capitalist system, is endeavouring to overthrow it, and also to public groups and organisations, under the influence of or directly organised by that bourgeoisie in conducting activities hostile to the USSR entails:

> deprivation of liberty for a period of not less than three years and confiscation of all or part of his property; to be increased in especially grave circumstances to the supreme measure of social defence – death by shooting, or declaration as an enemy of the toiling masses, coupled with deprivation of citizenship of the Union Republic and thereby of citizenship of the USSR, and banishment for ever beyond the frontiers of the USSR, and the confiscation of property.

Art. 58–5. Influencing a foreign State or any public groups within that State, by maintaining relations with its representatives, use of false documents or by any other means to a declaration of war, to armed intervention in the affairs of the USSR, or to any other hostile acts, in particular: to blockade, to seize the State property of the USSR or its Union Republics, to break off diplomatic relations, to break off agreements concluded with the USSR, etc. entails:

> measures of social defence enumerated in Article 58–2 of this Code.

Art. 58–6. Espionage, i.e. the transmission, theft or collection with a view to transmission to foreign States, counter-revolutionary organisations or private persons, of information accounted by reason of its contents an especially guarded State secret is punishable by:

> deprivation of liberty for a period of not less than three years, with confiscation of all or part of property; in cases, when espionage has caused, or might have caused, especially grievous consequences to the interests of the USSR the supreme measure of social defence – death by shooting, or the declaration to be an enemy of the labouring masses and the deprivation of citizenship of the Union Republic and thereby of the USSR and banishment beyond the frontiers of the USSR for ever, and confiscation of property.

The transmission, theft or collection with a view to transmission of economic information not constituting by virtue of its contents an especially guarded State secret but not intended for divulgence to the organisations or persons enumerated above, as the result of direct prohibition by law or by order of the heads of departments, establishments, or enterprises, either for recompense or gratis is punishable by:

deprivation of liberty for a period not exceeding three years.

Art. 58–7. The undermining of State industry, transport, trade, monetary exchange or the credit system and also of the co-operative network, committed for counter-revolutionary purposes by means of making use to such ends of State establishments and enterprises, or by means of impeding their normal functioning, and also the utilisation of State establishments and enterprises, or the impeding of their functioning in the interests of their former owners or of capitalist organisations interested in them is punishable by:

the measures of social defence, indicated in Article 58–2 of the present Code.

Art. 58–8. The commission of terrorist acts, directed against representatives of the Soviet regime or members of revolutionary workers' and peasants' organisations, and participation in the commission of such acts, even by persons not belonging to a counter-revolutionary organisation is punishable by:

the measures of social defence, indicated in Article 58–2 of the present Code.

Art. 58–9. The destruction or damage, for counter-revolutionary purposes, by explosives, arson or other means, of railways or other means of transportation, of the means of public communication, of water conduits, or public stores and other constructions or of State or public property, is punishable by:

the measures of social defence, indicated in Article 58–2 of the present Code.

Art. 58–10. Propaganda or agitation containing an appeal to overthrow, undermine or weaken the Soviet regime, or to commit individual counter-revolutionary crimes (Articles 58–2 to 58–9 of the present Code), and also the distribution, the preparation, or the conservation of literature of this nature, entails:

deprivation of liberty for a period of not less than six months.

Similar actions undertaken under conditions of mass unrest or involving the exploitation of the religious or national prejudices of the masses, or under conditions of war, or in localities placed under martial law are punishable by:

measures of social defence, indicated in Article 58–2 of the present Code.

Art. 58–11. Any type of organisational activity, directed towards the preparation or the commission of crimes provided for in the present chapter, and also participation in an organisation formed for the preparation or the commission of one of the crimes provided for in this chapter, is punishable by:

the measures of social defence, indicated in the relevant articles of the present chapter.

Art. 58–12. Failure to report reliable knowledge of preparations for, or commission of a counter-revolutionary crime entails:

deprivation of liberty for a period of not less than six months.

Art. 58–13. Actions or active struggle directed against the working class and the revolutionary movement, if committed by those in a responsible or secret (agent's) post under the Tsarist regime, or under counter-revolutionary Governments during the Civil War, are punishable by:

the measures of social defence indicated in Article 58–2 of the present Code.

Art. 58–14. Counter-revolutionary sabotage, i.e. deliberate non-fulfilment by anyone of duties laid down or the wilfully careless execution of those duties with a view to weakening the authority of the Government, the functioning of the State apparatus, entails:

> deprivation of liberty for a period of not less than one year, with confiscation of all or part of his property; to be increased in especially grave circumstances, to the supreme measure of social defence – death by shooting with confiscation of property.
> (Juridical Publishing House, Moscow, 1949.)

Index

Index

Abanya. Prisoner in Astrakhan and Saratov 44, 49, 63, 64, 69, 70, 71, 72
Action Group for the Defence of Human Rights in the USSR 16
Agapov, Sasha. Prisoner in Astrakhan 41, 44, 45, 47–8
Albert. Prisoner in Astrakhan 54–5, 59
Alksnis, Army Commander 27, 95
Altunyan, Genrikh 16, 17
Andrew, Father. Prisoner in Astrakhan 37
Anikeeva, Lyudmila Sergeevna. Counsellor at Verkhoturie 89, 90, 98, 100, 102
Astrakhan 28
Astrakhan prison 30, 35–62

BBK (White Sea–Baltic Camp complex) 75, 83, 128
Balashov transit prison 74–5
Batner, A. A. Military Jurist First Rank 94, 95
Bauman, Volodya. Prisoner in Verkhoturie 92, 101, 103
Belaya-Yakir, Isabella Emmanuilovna. Sister of General Yakir 86
Belov, Army Commander 27, 95
Benakh, Wanda. Prisoner at Nizhnyaya Tura 111–12
Bestuzhev ('Makhno'). Governor, Sevurallag 119, 121, 122, 123
Blyukher, Y. K. Marshal 27, 33, 95
Bogoslovsk. Section 14 of Sevurallag 116, 119
Bolshaya Kosalmanka labour camp. Part of Sevurallag 127, 136

Budyonny, S. M. Marshal 27, 95
Bukharina, Anna Mikhailevna (Nyusya) 29, 30, 86

Chadaev, Vakha. Prisoner at Sevurallag 118
Chelyabinsk prison 80–3
Chelyabinsk transit prison 78–80
Chervonets. Prisoner at Verkhoturie 91, 100
Children's Plot 11

Dugin. Manager. Nizhnyaya Tura 111–12
Dybenko, P. E. Army Commander 27, 95

Eideman, R. P. Corps Commander 27

Feldman, B. M. Corps Commander 27
Fomin. Deputy to Medved in Leningrad NKVD 93–4, 97
Frinovsky, Mikhail. NKVD Commissar 24, 25, 58, 94

Gamarnik, Blyuma Savelyevna 33, 34
Gamarnik, Yan Borisovich 33
Garkavaya, Emilia Lazarevna. P. Yakir's aunt 30, 42, 75
Garkavy, Ilya Ivanovich. Corps Commander 30, 93, 142
Garkavy, Volodya. P. Yakir's cousin 41, 75
Garkavy, Yura. P. Yakir's cousin 34, 41, 42, 44, 45, 48, 50, 52, 53–4, 59, 60, 61, 62, 64, 70, 71–2, 75

'Goldie'. Prisoner at Nizhnyaya Tura 106–7, 113, 115
Gorshorlag labour camp 110
Goryachov. Corps Commander 27, 95

Heliodor. Archimandrite of Tsaritsyn 36
'Hunchback'. Prisoner at Verkhoturie 115–16

'Imp'. Prisoner at Karelino 121
Ivan 'the Priest'. Prisoner in Astrakhan 43, 44, 45, 49
Ivanovich, Dmitri. Counsellor, Verkhoturie 99–100

Kaganovich, Lazar 143
Karelino. Camp 7 of Sevurallag 119, 130, 133, 138
Kartashov. Warden at Verkhoturie 89, 90, 98, 100, 101, 102
Kashirin. Army Commander 27, 95
Kashkin. Prisoner in Astrakhan 38–9
Kem labour camp 83
Khaikin, Abram. Prisoner in Astrakhan 40
Khrushchev, N. S. 12, 13, 144
Kiev 23
Kirov, Sergei M. 12, 93, 96, 97
Kolotilov, Ivan. Prisoner in Astrakhan 39–40
Komerstein Vera Alexandrovna. Wife of S. I. Sapronov 25
Kork, A. I. Head of Frunze Military Academy 27, 142
Korzuby, Kostya. Prisoner in Saratov, 66, 68, 69, 71
Kossior, S. V. 26
Kungur Labour Commune 89
Kupchik. Chief of Kiev NKVD Special Branch 26
Kurilko. Commandant Solovki Islands Camp 109
Kurtz, Gottlieb Eduardovich 126

Lekhem. Chief of Astrakhan NKVD 35, 53
Lyosha. Prisoner at Verkhoturie and Nizhnyaya Tura 106, 107, 113, 115

Markaryan, Natasha 30, 86
Malaya Kosalmanka labour camp. Part of Sevurallag 126–7
Marusya. Leader of Verkhoturie Pioneer Group 98, 102
Mashka. Prisoner in Astrakhan and Saratov 44, 46, 63, 66
Medved, Philip. Leningrad NKVD chief 92, 93, 97
Medved, Mischa. Son of P. Medved. Prisoner in Verkhoturie and Sevurallag 92, 98, 100, 102, 105, 106, 108, 112, 114, 115, 116, 126
Medvezhia Gora labour camp 83, 128
Mischka 'The Stallion'. Prisoner in Bolshaya Kosalmanka 131, 132
Molotov, V. M. 13, 143
Moskovkin. NKVD interrogator 31, 34, 35, 41, 53, 56–7

Nekrich, A. M. Historian 14
Nikolayev, Leonid. Kirov's assassin 92, 93–4
Nizhnyaya Tura Maximum Security Colony 103–116
Nosalevsky. Secretary Astrakhan City Komsomol Committee 56–7

Ortenberg, Lazar Petrovich. P. Yakir's maternal grandfather 28, 31, 42, 45–6, 47, 48, 53, 62, 102
Otto. Governor at Nizhnyaya Tura 105, 115

Parandovo labour camp 83
Peterson, A. A. 26n.
Peterson, Ira. Daughter of A. A. Peterson 25

Petrov. Camp security officer, Verkhoturie 115–16
Petrov, Colonel 137–8
Pletnyov, Dimitry 67
Pogrebinsky. NKVD chief for Gorky region 89
Preobrazhensky, Pyotr Fyodorovich 125
Preobrazhensky, Sergei Fyodorovich. Prisoner at Sevurallag 124–6, 127, 129, 133, 135–6, 138
Primakov, V. M. Corps Commander 27, 95
Prorvlag labour camp 58–9
Putna, V. K. Corps Commander 27, 141, 142

Radek, Sonia. Daughter of Karl Radek 42, 46, 47

Sapronov, Sergei Ivanovich 25, 27
Sapronov, Yura 25n
Saratov 64
Saratov prison 65–73
Sasha 'the Yid'. Prisoner at Sevurallag 117
Segezha labour camp 83
Sevurallag labour camp system 98, 116, 134–5
Shaposhnikov. Army Commander 27, 95
Shavan labour camp 83
Shmidt, Dmitri. Divisional Commander 141, 142
Shorokh. Deputy chief Kiev NKVD Special Branch 26
Slava. Uborevich's nephew 42, 47, 48, 53
Sokolovsky. Doctor. Prisoner in Syzran 76
Solovki Islands labour camp 109
Sosva. Sevurallag Administration Centre 136
Stalin, Josef 12, 13, 14, 15, 18, 52, 78, 85, 93, 94, 95, 96, 97, 130, 141, 142, 143, 144
Stepanchenko, Sergei. Prisoner at Nizhnyaya Tura 109, 110, 111

Sverdlovsk 83, 138
Sverdlovsk prison 84, 86–8, 91
Syzran transit prison 76–8

Third Watershed labour camp 83
Tukhachevsky, Mikhail Nikolayevich. Marshal 12, 13, 23, 27, 33, 142
Tukhachevsky, Nina Evgenyevna 33, 34

UChPP labour camp 83
USLON. Solovki Islands Administration of Special Purposes Camps 83
Uborevich, Y. P. Army Commander 27, 33, 95
Ukhov, Kolya. Prisoner in Verkhoturie 92, 101, 103
Ulrikh, V. V. Chairman. Military Collegium of the Supreme Court 27, 95, 96

Vasya 'The Beast'. Prisoner at Nizhnyaya Tura 113
Vasyok. Prisoner at Sevurallag 117
Verkhoturie Disciplinary Colony for Juveniles 89–103
Voroshilov, Kliment. People's Commissar for Defence 13, 23, 97, 141, 143, 144

'Wizard'. Prisoner at Nizhnyaya Tura 107

Yagoda, Genrikh. Chief of NKVD 89, 93
Yakir, Irina. P. Yakir's daughter 18, 19
Yakir, Ion Emmanuilovich 11, 17, 23, 27, 33, 94–5, 141–4
Yakir, Mrs 23–31, 42, 86
Yenukidze, Pyotr 120
Yuzhny labour camp 83

Zaporozhets, Leonid. NKVD official 97
Zhukov, I. P. Marshal 13